"As a prominent voice in the world of college admission, Dr. Cynthia Colón's advice to high school students is spot on! Every student who dreams of going to college should read this book — it's funny, entertaining and informative. After reading *Tips, Tales & Truths* for Teens, I have no doubt students and parents will be begging her for even more words of wisdom!"

–SARAH GALLAGHER DVORAK,
Director of Admission at Saint Mary's College in Notre Dame, IN

"Youth across the nation need a cheerleader and guide to help them build their high school college application over four years. Dr. Cynthia Colón provides *Tips, Tales and Truths* in a fun and tangible format. As a first generation college graduate and a former guidance counselor, she offers vulnerability, transparency and veracity about the college admission process. The reader can hear Dr. Colón cheering emphatically through the words on the pages for youth to find their passion and their own leadership voice on this journey to achieve their own "impossible" dream."

–DR. ERIN BRUNNER RICHISON
Former High School Principal
Principal Coach, San Diego County Office of Education

"Dr. Colón draws on her rich professional experience to deliver a dynamic guidebook to help navigate what at times can be a daunting and Byzantine experience for high school students and their families. Possessing the credibility and unique perspective of someone who has spent time as both a high school college counselor as well as an admissions officer in one of the most selective institutions in higher education, *Tips, Tales & Truths* stands as a powerful roadmap that should be required reading for all students who are planning on going to college, but are just unsure quite how to get there."

–MR. CASEY YEAZEL
Principal, St. John Bosco High School
President, VSM Education Consulting

"Cynthia Colón's journey and mine have a similar trajectory. Both of us came from families with limited resources and were first generation college students. Both of us worked at fine academic institutions. It was at USC that I had the good fortune to meet Cynthia and to watch her flourish and grow during her college years. Her college experience gave root to her desire to give back. Her work in admissions assisted many students to reach their dreams and now she is taking that experience and desire to give back in writing *Tips, Tales & Truths*. Cynthia "walks the talk" and shares "words of wisdom" gleaned from her experiences in an easy to read and edifying book for teens aspiring to reach their college dreams and beyond."

–DR. CYNTHIA CHERREY
International Leadership Association President and CEO
Former Vice President for Campus Life, Princeton University
Former Vice President for Student Affairs, Tulane University

"Working in Student Affairs, I interact with hundreds of students and families each year as they are making their final decisions about whether to attend our university, and I can see that for many, they still don't have a clear strategy about how to make that choice. Dr. Colon's book will help students map their priorities well in advance of that deadline for making this major decision. While the book helps students approach the college admission process intentionally, I like that *Tips, Tales & Truths* encourages students to be reflective and genuine, rather than simply providing a checklist to follow."

–JAYNE E. BROWNELL, ED.D.
Vice President for Student Affairs, Miami University

"Running a youth leadership organization and working with hundreds of teenagers each year, *Tips Tales & Truths* provides great lessons about how to succeed in the college process and in life. Dr. Cynthia Colón shows how anything is possible with a plan. This book is filled with heartfelt stories that will inspire the best in everyone. A must read for all teens and parents!"

–HEIDI MCNIFF JOHNSON
Executive Director TACSC A Catholic Youth Leadership Organization

"Having read Dr. Colón's book my only regret is she didn't put her lessons to print a decade earlier when our oldest child began her college application journey! Though we got better with each iteration (we have 4 children) we were never as good as we could have been if only we'd had Cynthia's work to guide us. The perfect gift for every new High School Freshman, *Tips, Tales & Truths* is filled with the passion and wisdom I've had the pleasure to personally witness in one of the best leaders and mentors I know... Dr. Cynthia Colón"

–KEVIN P. CHILTON
General (ret) USAF and former NASA Astronaut

"Dr. Colón is the warm, wise college counselor every teen needs. The insider tips, tales and truths in her book guide readers through the college admission process with authenticity and control."

–MARY E. MANSELL
Principal, Ramona Convent Secondary School

"Dr. Colón's new book, *Tips, Tales & Truths*, is a treasure trove and provides a wealth of information not only for the high school student navigating the sometimes complicated maze in the college admissions world but also for the student's parents and high school counselor. The book's format and content are easily assessable and read with the energy reflective of its author. Dr. Colón's experience, dynamism, and passion jump out at you as you read this valuable resource. I highly recommend this book and encourage you to tell fellow students, teachers and counselors about this wonderful addition to your personal library."

–MONSIGNOR SAL PILATO, KM, KCHS, MA, MDIV
Superintendent of High Schools, 2008-2017, Archdiocese of Los Angeles

TIPS, TALES & TRUTHS

for Teens

A former college admission officer and
private school counselor shares
real stories and candid advice about the
plan to apply to college.

DR. CYNTHIA COLÓN

TIPS, TALES & TRUTHS
FOR TEENS

Cover Design & Layout by Juan Pablo Ruiz
Printed in the United States of America

ISBN: 978-0-9971605-4-3

FIG
FACTOR
MEDIA

Dedicated to
my biggest cheerleaders
and grandest believers,
Mom and Dad

YOUR GRAND PLAN:

ACKNOWLEDGEMENTS

Thank you, a thousand times, thank you!

To My Team of Supporters: Mom and Jess, I love you both more than you know. As my life took a turn, you supported my desire to take a journey into the unknown. I will forever be thankful for your unconditional love and support. To the Colón cousins and my nieces and one little nephew, thank you for bringing me so much joy throughout this past year. To the Franco familia, I am so glad there are so many Francos from which to choose character names from. You just might find yourself in the book. Cheers!

To My Village of Cheerleaders: The women and men of Marymount have been my village for seventeen years. I started working at Marymount when I was only 27 years old and left just before turning 40. It is because of my village of cheerleaders that I learned to lead humbly while empowering new student leaders. It is because of Jill, Judy, Sharon, Debra, Sandy, Mary Ellen, and Kathleen that Marymount served as my training ground to eventually take on my own leadership role. Many of my colleagues I now count as friends. Thank you Dorothy, Delia, Marie, Amie, Traci, Lyndsey, Kathy, Vikki, Amy, Sally, MaryAnn, Valerie, Marilyn, Kim, Chris, Patrick, and Patrick for always being my village of cheerleaders.

To My Community of Believers: I have always looked beyond the ordinary and seen the possibilities in people and situations. Once I get an idea in my head, I begin to share it with others. Like selling something that does not yet exist, it takes a special person to buy into an idea at the early onset. Author and business pundit Simon Sinek calls these people early adopters; I call them believers. Everyone needs a community of believers, for it is lonely to dream alone.

A special thank you to: Jess, Kristin, Tía Gloria, Sheetal, Natalie, Franca, Jonas, Sarah and Todd, Daniel and Lynne, Michelle and Geoff, Courtney and DiAnthony, Joan and Richard, Luisa, Gail, Alice, Mary, Sean, Casey, Christian, Chris, Kevin, Mari, Ross, and Tosh.

To Amie Kosberg, thank you for your enthusiastic support, your friendship, and your genuine belief in me. I am grateful for your assistance in reviewing the manuscript and candid feedback along the way. You are my life-long friend.

To Jayne Brownell, on July 1, 2016, I began what I fondly call my "Lemonade Tour" and drove through ten states in 31 days, and over 4000 miles. Who knew that 20 years after meeting each other in New York City, we would be living together in Oxford, Ohio! Thank you for opening up your home and allowing me to cover the basement with posters and color-coded post-its, each containing a tip, tale, or truth. You were one of the very first to believe that I could and would write a book, and for that I am eternally thankful. Love you much! How about next time we meet in NYC or LA? Drinks on me!

INTRODUCTION: IT'S GO-TIME

"Nothing is Impossible, the word itself says, 'I'm Possible'!"
– Audrey Hepburn

My right shoulder pressed the phone against my ear as I tore open the envelope from the University of Southern California and read it to my mother who took my call while at her desk at Security Pacific National Bank. "Dear Ms. Cyndie Colón, It is with great pleasure that I welcome you to the class of 1994 . . . " I didn't get much past the first sentence when I dropped the phone and ran around the house screaming, crying, and laughing. That night, Mom and I celebrated with two scoops of ice cream.

The truth is, my parents did not attend college. I went through high school without a clear plan on what to do, and by senior year, I had no clue where to find a college application, let alone how to apply. In spite of this, I was admitted to my first choice school. How, you ask? Serendipity? My charming personality? I was lucky enough to have parents who taught me that anything is possible. My father was a dreamer of big ideas and passed on his incredible creativity to me. At the same time, my mother was practical and logical; she knew dreams could be achieved more easily with a college degree. Mom never questioned if I would go to college but rather where. With their support, I was a doer in high school and managed to have good grades, a nice resume, cool leadership qualities, and I took the necessary exams. That year, I was the only student from Bellflower High School to attend USC. What I know now is this–times have changed since I applied to college. If I applied today under the same circumstances (without a plan), it just might be *impossible* to get in.

After USC, I set out to become an educator, a champion of students. I traveled across the country to learn from the best at Teachers College, Columbia University. My family could not afford to travel with me when I moved to New York City to study at Columbia, but they were there in force at graduation. During their week long visit, I rode with my mother on the train along the Hudson River to visit the campus where I landed my first job offer–Vassar College in upstate New York. Our taxi entered through what seemed like the archway to a brick castle, and in an instant, there we stood like two bright dots against the monochromatic backdrop of Main Building. "If you don't take this job, I will," my mom said. Her eyes were wide with disbelief of the beauty of the campus staring back at us.

My time at Vassar introduced me to students from around the country. As an admission officer, I learned about private schools and heard the term "elite" for the first time. My territory included California and places I'd never been before, like Florida, Texas, Kansas, Minnesota, and the Dakotas. Meeting students and their families was my favorite part of the job, and most of them had a clear plan for getting admitted to college. I longed to find students for whom I could champion in the admissions committee. I had my share of wins and heartbreaks, but I learned that the process of decision-making in the admissions office is not plain and simple but rather complex and difficult. It was not long before I decided it would be *impossible* for me to spend my days denying more students than admitting.

Having grown up with nine aunts, I found my home at the elite all-girls school, Marymount High School in Los Angeles. As the Director of College Counseling, I could share my knowledge from my East Coast experience and add value to conversations with families about their daughters' college options. Many families had more resources than I could ever imagine, and with my assistance, we created a grand plan for applying to colleges. Nothing seemed *impossible* for these young women. As often as my life seemed an ocean apart from theirs, the truth is that every high school student, no matter their background, has the same hopes, dreams, joys, fears, and worries as any other teenager. This was an insightful lesson to learn before the age of 30. For this, I am incredibly thankful to the amazing young women I encountered every day for twelve years.

In many ways, those girls inspired me to chase my own dreams and become an entrepreneur. I joined with a colleague and formed Co-Ed College Consultants, Inc. This small business was created with one mission: to help as many students as possible write their best college admission essays. What once seemed *impossible* turned into a dream come true. The company continued until I began my dissertation work at the University of California, Los Angeles, in the fall of 2008.

By the age of 39, I had achieved nearly everything I set out to do in high school, my adult life, and in my career. I attended and worked at some of the finest colleges in the country. Between the ages of 19 and 39, I traveled to seven countries and more than 20 states, all in the name of college football, work, the World Cup, and culture. I climbed the career ladder, started a small business, got married, and became the first in my extended family to earn a doctorate degree. Dr. Colón had achieved the nearly *impossible*.

But in April of 2012, for the first time in my life, I sat without a clue as to what was in front of me. After eight interviews as a finalist for principal, I had not received a single offer; I was running out of hope. My dream of leading a school and inspiring hundreds of students just might be *impossible*.

It took several more conversations, but by mid-June, I was offered the job as principal of St. Bernard High School. I had no idea what a job offer would sound like, but coming from Monsignor Pilato, it was delivered more like a calling rather than a choice. I can assure you that this assignment was the most challenging and exhilarating time in my life. With financial instability, decreasing enrollment, broken windows, run down buildings, and no Wi-Fi, the task seemed literally impossible to all stakeholders. Not me. I believed in giving the students what they deserved, and I began a mission to help them dream the *impossible*.

This book is about achieving the *impossible*, whatever that means to you. It is about believing in yourself, learning from mistakes, and believing there is a plan—a college—that is just for you. In order to achieve the impossible, you must understand that you are in control of this process, something I did not know in 1990 but that I am fully aware of now.

I do not purport to have all the answers; I am a product of my own journey and life lessons. What I offer are 33 tips, tales, and truths for you to ponder and apply to your own journey.

Each chapter is divided into three easy-to-read parts:

TIP

This recommendation comes from wearing my college-counseling hat. I am the voice of your counselor, advisor, and mentor all in one.

TALE

Many students I have met from around the country have inspired these mini-dramas I call tales. Each tale offers a unique story inspired by real students. Some tales are from my own high school experience, where I was known as Cyndie. Others are from my encounters with students while I served as the college counselor or dean of students. In these instances, I was called Ms. Colón. Those tales told from the voice of a college admission officer, I am known simply as Cynthia. And finally, the recounted stories from Dr. Colón are those from my days as principal. Most tales take place at one of my favorite schools: Bellflower High School, Marymount High School, Vassar College, or St. Bernard High School.

TRUTH

This section is my candid advice as a veteran college admission officer. I offer the truth as my advice on what you can take away from the tale and a reminder of what you do have control over in the college admission process.

Tips, Tales & Truths is laid out in seven chapters, each designed to offer a specific plan on how you can manage this seemingly unwieldy process. While I recommend reading them in order, it is easy to go through the table of contents and find a tip you may need for motivation today.

CHAPTER 1: Your Four-Year Plan

Whether you are the first in your family to attend college, have siblings in college, or your parents graduated from an Ivy League institution, applying to college is new to YOU. I want you to shoot for the moon. This chapter offers a plan of how to get there.

CHAPTER 2: Your Pre-Application Plan

Believe it or not, ninety percent of the college application happens before you reach senior year. This chapter offers clear and easy tips to add to your to-do list. If you can make these suggestions part of your routine, you will control this process more than you can possibly realize.

CHAPTER 3: Your Resume Plan

Look up, look out, and try everything. Whether your interests lie in clubs, service, sports, performing arts, or competitive organizations, the message here is to do something at your school. This chapter is a reminder that interested students make for interesting applicants.

CHAPTER 4: Your Leadership Plan

Do what is right. Listen to others. Utilize your passions. Leave a legacy. This chapter offers examples of how real students found their authentic why, and once they did, how they thrived as leaders.

CHAPTER 5: Your Self-Improvement Plan

This chapter offers real stories of students who pushed themselves to learn from mistakes, show courage, and become self-advocates. You are resilient. You are amazing beyond your imagination. You are in control of you.

CHAPTER 6: Your Senior Year Plan

Give 1000 percent to what you control, and you will have no regrets. This chapter offers a step-by-step process for building your list of colleges, how to choose your essay topic, how to ask your teachers for recommendations, and how to relieve stress while waiting for college responses.

CHAPTER 7: Your New Plan Awaits

This chapter is a homage to the month of April that comes in senior year. I offer a variety of mini-dramas highlighting the joy, fear, disappointment, worry, confusion, and elation that comes with receiving admission decisions. This is an exciting time in your life; celebrate every single victory along the way!

Oh and one last thing . . .

My hope is that you will not only read *Tips, Tales & Truths* but go back and reference the bigger ideas that somehow shifted something inside you when you first read them. Every stage of your life journey is different. So keep this book handy. Many of the lessons apply to life beyond high school when you are heading into college graduation and pursuing a career.

High school represents the most formidable years of

your life. You will achieve great things, you will fail, you will make great choices, and you will make mistakes. You will form lasting friendships, you will be disappointed, you will find your confidence, and you will often doubt yourself. You will fall in love, you will have your heart broken, and you will find yourself because of these events. Balancing all of the above, while also having to think about your future, is a lot to ask for of any teenager. It can be overwhelming, I know. But, I promise, nothing about the college admission process is *impossible*. You, more than anyone else, can make it possible.

Now let's get to it!

Dr. Cynthia Colón

CHAPTER 1

YOUR FOUR-YEAR PLAN

TIP #1: This process begins with a dream and the College Counseling Office. Get there early and often.

TALE:
My Dream Weighed Less Than Eight Ounces

When I was in high school, I painted my room yellow. I watched Trojan football every Saturday, and my favorite Christmas gift was my first USC sweatshirt from my bestie, Jess. Neither of my parents had attained a college degree, but my father's love for watching the Trojan Marching Band perform on the football field at halftime, sparked my dream of becoming a cardinal-and-gold-wearing USC student. My mother attended community college and had plans of becoming a flight attendant. She was only twenty years old when my arrival stunted her dreams. While my mother knew I was infatuated with USC, it was not until November of my senior year that she understood my plight.

After working an early shift at Moffett's Family Restaurant, I was home just in time to watch the USC v. UCLA game. My sisters were with Dad for the day, and I yelled out, "Hi, Mom." I bundled up on the couch to watch the game with my cozy Trojan blanket made by Tía Irma (Tía is Spanish for aunt). Mom had no interest in sports, but she joined me at halftime.

"What's up Ladybug? You've been quiet all week," with a warm quesadilla in hand, it was a great way to get me to talk.

"Everyone at school is talking about college. Applications are due after Christmas break." I took my first bite and the cheese oozed out onto my hand.

"Yeah, and? You are applying too." I paused before responding.

"I picked up the applications for all the state schools, but the office did not have one for USC. I don't think I'll apply anyway," I stared at the television. It had been two years since my father moved out and mom was left to raise three children on a single income.

"Ladybug, I never had a chance to follow my dreams, but…" Before she finished I asked, "But how would we pay for it?" She smiled and cried at the same time, "We will figure it out, Ladybug. We always do."

The following week was a whirlwind, and my mother was on a mission. She knew nothing about applying to college, how to pay for college, or even how to get a USC application. Mom called Tía Gloria who was a school principal who told my mother to call the counseling office at my high school and insist on an appointment right away. Mom followed the exact advice, and within 24 hours, we had an appointment. My mom may not have had a degree, but in that week, she became my superhero.

Mom took a half-day from work and met me on a Thursday after school. Mr. Vargas, whom I had only met once before, greeted my mother "Mrs. Colón, so good to meet you. We think Cyndie is doing a great job as student body president." His big smile warmed the room. Mr. Vargas offered tips for my application to USC, and more than that, he carefully explained to my mother how it was possible to pay for college with financial aid and scholarship assistance. He made sure we understood all of the deadlines, and he had an application ready for me on the way out. Mr. Vargas could make no promises, but he was encouraging nonetheless. Before I left his office, we set an appointment to meet again two weeks later.

Hindered by my own fear of not getting in, I let that application sit on the dining room table. Two weeks later, I sat in Mr. Vargas' office with nothing to report. I sat, head hung low, waiting for him to scold me as if I had ditched class. To my surprise, Mr. Vargas rolled his chair directly in front of mine. My eyes only rose up to stare back at his white beard and face with the wrinkles of a wise man. "What's the matter, Cyndie?" Like Santa Claus, Mr. Vargas whispered the words, inviting me to share why I wasn't doing anything to pursue the one Christmas gift I wanted more than anything else.

"USC is my dream school. What if I don't get in?" I tried to hold back the tears, but one escaped down my cheek.

Santa Claus waited for me to look up at him, "You'll never know unless you apply."

With that twinkle in his eye, I knew he was right. The

next 24 hours was another whirlwind. I drafted my essay, completed the application, and picked up my sealed letters of recommendation from Mr. Vargas. On Tuesday after school, I walked to the post office, had the lady weigh my package, and paid for the postage.

My dream weighed less than eight ounces.

TRUTH:

Navigating the college admissions process is unwieldy for any teenager. Whether you are the first in your family to attend college, have siblings in college, or your parents graduated from an Ivy League institution, applying to college is new to YOU. And because YOU have never been through this process, I am here to help you make a plan.

The first step is to get in there and meet your counselor. Do not wait to have a problem with a teacher or your schedule, and do not wait until you get in trouble because you were tardy or ditched a class (by accident). The counselor is a key ingredient to your success in school and in the application process, so grab an apple or make a batch of cookies and swing by to introduce yourself. With this small effort s/he will remember who you are among a sea of teenagers.

Depending on the size of your high school, it can take

"The counselor is a key ingredient to your success in school and in the application process, so grab an apple or make a batch of cookies and swing by to introduce yourself."

some time to reach a counselor and/or set up an appointment. If the office is such that you cannot just stop in, I recommend making friends with the receptionist and requesting a 15-minute appointment with your counselor for the following week. The goal as a freshman is simple: introduce yourself, ask a few questions (about schedule, college, study tips), and leave a small token of appreciation so you are remembered. That's it.

Getting to know your counselor will be the best investment you can make in yourself.

TIP #2: Take Control. You control this process — don't ever believe otherwise.

TALE:

Shoot For The Moon, But Make A Plan To Get There

"I'm sorry, Mr. Fisher, I know we haven't met, but I don't have Melissa's file. Are you sure she is not assigned to another college counselor?"

"No, I'm sorry, Ms. Colón. Melissa is going to be a sophomore, she hasn't been assigned at all."

Confused, I continued, "I see. Did you still want to come in this summer?"

"Yes, if you have time, we could come in next week." With that, we set a date to meet.

Mr. Fisher had one agenda item: to get his daughter into the best college possible. Ivy League was his preference.

Melissa and Mr. Fisher showed up on time, and he proceeded to do most of the talking. I often turned my attention to the right, where she sat quietly. "Melissa, what is it that you like to do? Want to do? What do you see yourself excelling in over the next three years?" She answered each question in the same tone – not overly enthusiastic, but not disinterested either. As the oldest child, she would be the first to apply to college and traverse the muddy waters of highly selective institutions. Mr. and Mrs. Fisher had both attended college in California, but in the last few years it was no secret the landscape of college admissions had significantly changed.

Melissa talked about enjoying student council. As a freshman, she was involved in a variety of clubs, and at the end of the year, she ran for class council and won. She would lead the sophomores as their class president when school began in just three weeks. "OK, this is good information, Melissa. And where do you dream of attending college?"

Before she could answer, Mr. Fisher chimed in, "We are looking at all the Ivies."

Without acknowledging Mr. Fisher, I kept my focus to my right "Is this true, Melissa? Is that what you want?"
Mr. Fisher did not dare interrupt again, and, as if she finally recognized that I was her advocate, Melissa sat up straight and showed me her hazel eyes "Brown and Columbia are my favorites, but I love UCLA too." With a small grin, she added, "Call me Missy." I smiled back and winked.

"The academic profile of a student is the most important element."

Together, the three of us spent the next 50 minutes brainstorming and creating a backwards map. With no guarantees of landing on the moon, we forged ahead. The academic profile of a student is the most important element. Missy would need to be eligible to take four or five advanced placement (AP) courses in her senior year, which meant taking three in junior year that naturally advanced into the next set of APs. I was happy to hear that Melissa had already been assigned to the only AP offered to sophomores, AP European History.

This young lady with the round face, hazel eyes, and straight brown hair was already on her way. She asked questions about the SAT exams, which teachers she might consider getting letters of recommendation from, the necessary grades, and of course her resume. Missy's eyes danced when she spoke of class council, "I think I would like to run for student body president at the end of junior year."

Without hesitation I simply asked, "Just like taking AP Euro is the best move for getting into AP US History, what do you think is the best strategic position to have as a junior to enable you to run for student council president?"

Missy verbalized all of the possibilities and options with an understanding of the political ramifications at an all-girls school; the key was to stay active and visible without hogging all the star leadership roles. Being class president two years in a row would almost guarantee that these savvy girls would vote to give a different student a chance to lead. After 90 minutes of game planning and strategizing, the Fisher family left very happy. In Missy's desire to shoot for the moon, making a plan was the easy part. Working her plan meant hard work, late nights, redrafting term papers, after-school practice, weekend commitments, and the courage to persevere no matter what. *That* was the hard part.

I know you want to know, so I will tell you this, Missy went on to attend Brown University, which is the good news. The GREAT news is this, she followed her plan almost exactly the way we laid it out on that summer day, and most importantly her academic curriculum and grades were nearly perfect. She did run and won the role of student council president. In addition to being a leader on the winning Model United Nations and track teams, Missy also spoke off campus as the lead ambassador of the school. The summer before her final year, she drafted her college essay six times. She was committed to her dreams and climbed every inch of that mountain to get there. In September of her senior year, Missy did not know where she would be twelve months later, but she knew this, she had taken control of this process early on, and she alone was responsible for every decision along the way.

TRUTH:

As a college admission officer, I was always surprised to watch how worked up students were about the college admission process. With time came clarity, and I understand now that this process can make sane people spin out of control solely because s/he believes they have

"The truth is, you have control over everything that goes into that college application."

no control. Have no fear. The truth is, you have control over everything that goes into that college application. Yes, I did say everything. Like Missy, with a little planning, you can create a road map as early as the summer before freshman or sophomore year and become armed and ready for that senior year application.

Disclosure: not everyone is going to land on the moon. In fact, it takes many stars to align perfectly to receive a "big" envelope from one of the top 20 most selective institutions in the country, but the point here is that it can happen and it does happen. The lessons to glean from Melissa's story are two-fold: plan an academic path that is rigorous and realistic, and build a resume that demonstrates the breadth and depth of your talents and leadership. Remember this, when you shoot for the moon, sometimes you actually get there.

TIP #3: Like a treadmill, grades should have an incline not a decline.

TALE:
High School Is Your Training Ground For The Marathon Of College

For eight weeks between September and November, I earned sky miles and hotel points, met hundreds of parents and students, and visited dozens of high schools. This was the marathon that admission officers called "Fall Recruiting Season." While most students were in their senior year, many guests were already previewing colleges as sophomores and juniors. Those were the families who asked questions that piqued my interest and continued to follow me even more once I became a high school college counselor. After my presentation in the school gym or a hotel ballroom, a line would form with skirt-and-tie wearing young women and men with parents in tow. As one family left, the next introduced themselves, "Hello, Cynthia, nice to meet you. I wanted to ask, is it better to get an A in a regular course or a B in an honors or advanced placement (AP) course?" At first I was stumped by this question, and I am positive I stumbled in my answer the first time. It did not occur to me that this child was asking for permission to enroll in the less challenging course. Never once did I fall for that trap.

The short answer to the stated question is this, it is better to take the more challenging course.

However, there are two things wrong with this question. First, as you plot and plan your academic curriculum every spring, your journey should reflect an increase in rigor. Think of it this way, you do not go to the gym and walk one mile on the treadmill forever, do you? No, you increase the time, the pace, and the incline. And even when it seems like you can barely breathe after 15 minutes, you push yourself to go two more minutes again and again. Before you know it, you have gone from walking one mile to running a 5K. Voila! The same goes for school. Each year you should increasingly challenge your brain and remember that you are training for the marathon you call college. The more you can train in high school, the better prepared you will be for the taxing demands of your college professors. I had to learn the hard way that you cannot write a good 15-page paper overnight.

The second problem inherent in the aforementioned question is that you should not set yourself up for settling for a B. I believe in self-fulfilling prophecy: say it out loud and it becomes your truth. I took a small group communication course in college, and, you guessed it, we had to work in small groups. We named our team "Frosted

"It is always best to shoot for the A in the honors or Advanced Placement course. Period."

Flakes," and I think you probably can guess how we worked; we were flaky and the professor called us out on it. The moment you tell yourself that the best grade you can achieve is X, then you have already set yourself up to do mediocre work that will satisfy the stated goal. With that said, enter high school with the belief that you can achieve the best grades possible with hard work, dedication, and a commitment to having no regrets.

The real answer is, it is always best to shoot for the A in the honors or advanced placement course. Period.

TRUTH:

The adults in your life often think back, wonder, and wish they had done better in high school. He reminisces about how smart he was, while she knows she could have studied or read more. It is no wonder that many parents spend time pushing their own kids to do just that, because they know how much potential you have.

Let me take a moment to reinforce this truth: you have complete control over the admission process. You do not want to get to senior year with regrets, especially in the academic department. I am not suggesting that one must always earn straight As. In fact, what I am suggesting is simple: give it your 110 percent and you will never regret it. This could mean the difference between a B+ or A- or could mean a B instead of a C. I have seen more students wish they had a stronger academic record than I can count, and the truth is they have nobody to blame but themselves.

For the very elite colleges, yes, you will need a perfect or nearly perfect transcript to get your foot in the door. Most colleges, however, simply want to see a challenging curriculum, an upward trend in grades, and someone who is ready for the demanding academic life that surprises many in college.

Bottom line, no matter where you are from, which high school you attend, and what your resources are, your goal should always be for the pace of your grades to be on a steady incline and never a decline. With that said, academic life does not come naturally easy for everyone. Do not beat yourself up over a couple of lower grades in your freshman year. The message here is to get back on that treadmill and keep training. Soon you are physically and mentally stronger, your second wind kicks in, and you discover your optimum performance. You will race to the finish line. I promise, you got this!

TIP #4: Given YOUR resources, what are you doing to optimally utilize them?

TALE:
A Dream Delayed Finally Takes Flight

Mr. Simmons worked at Los Angeles International Airport (LAX) marshaling planes in every day. Michael Simmons was a seventh grade participant when I met his father at the annual Science, Technology, Engineering, and Mathematics (STEM) Summit conference. Mr. Simmons stood at the back of the room as Michael ran over to show him the medal that bore a Viking ship. Mr. Simmons pointed at his son and whispered, "Guion," a code word only known to Michael.

Two years later, I directed freshman and sophomore parents and students to the front of the hall on College Night. I spotted Michael, "Good to see you, where is your father?" Pointing in his father's direction, "Dr. Colón, he is in the back." I found my veteran parent, Mr. Jackson, and watched him work his magic. Mr. Jackson nonchalantly walked to the back of the room and invited Mr. Simmons to join him and Mrs. Jackson.

Mr. and Mrs. Jackson had a senior daughter headed to

Marquette University. Their son Bryce was a sophomore. It wasn't long before Michael found himself nearly adopted by the Jacksons. The Jackson family lived near the campus, and Michael often went over after school for a snack before football or soccer practice or hung out after an all-day workday for robotics. One afternoon, Michael inquired about Shelia Jackson and Marquette University. Shelia had built quite a resume highlighting her leadership in community service, student council, and with her youth group. Marquette, along with several other colleges, offered Shelia partial scholarships, Mrs. Jackson explained, which made college more affordable for her family. It was those conversations at the Jackson home that inspired Michael to dream about college.

By the time Michael was a junior, he was the lead engineer on the robotics team and selected as the director of STEM Summit. Michael poured his energy into reading and researching topics like engineering, programming, and building a robot from scratch. Throughout the fall, Michael networked with the adults from The Aerospace Corporation when they were on campus and asked where they went to school, what they majored in, and about work and internships. He learned about Olin College of Engineering, MIT, and RIT, and others closer to home like, Cal Poly, SLO, Harvey Mudd, and the prestigious Cal Tech. One of the top executives of Aerospace took a liking to Michael and offered him a part-time job at the plant the summer before his senior year. His STEM resume was impeccable; he had taken advantage of every opportunity afforded to him in three plus years, and all that was left was to apply to college.

In addition to working at Aerospace on Saturdays, Michael spent most of his summer studying for the SAT. Each morning, Michael woke up at six in the morning to have breakfast with his father before they each went off to work. By 6:30 a.m., Mr. Simmons put on his vest and with his forefinger, touched his son's heart and whispered, "Guion." This was their code word for dreams. Mr. Simmons had named his son Michael Guion as a tribute to his hero, Guion Bluford, the first African American in space. Mr. Simmons had once dreamed of becoming an aeronautical engineer but left college early to raise Michael on his own.

Michael applied to six engineering programs, and by April he received congratulations from three. In the end, it was ultimately the co-op program at Rochester Institute of Technology that won him over. Mr. Simmons' dream may have been delayed, but that August his son finally took flight and traveled across the country to Rochester, NY, sight unseen. Four years later, "Guion" earned his wings and became the first college graduate in his family.

TRUTH:

If you take nothing else away from this book, consider one question, "Given YOUR resources, what are you doing to optimally utilize them?" As an admission officer, I tended to use this as a good litmus test: something I learned from JC Tesone at Vassar College.

What does this look like? I'll give you an academic example. If your high school offers two advanced placement (AP) courses and you take both, then that shows the reader that you have taken the most demanding course load offered.

"The truth is no matter what your background, the college application process will require you to have encouragers, realists, gentle pushers, cheerleaders, and mentors."

On the other hand, if the top students at your high school are graduating with eight AP courses, and you have taken two, then the list of colleges you have as options is much different than the kid who took the most demanding curriculum made available to him/her.

Do yourself a favor. If your parents attended college, pick their brains, talk to their friends, learn about different careers and fields. Find what interests you, and take their advice. For those of you with siblings in college or recently graduated, inquire about courses they took for different majors, ask what they wish they had done, learned, or read in high school to better prepare them for college. Your siblings and their friends have a wealth of information; utilize them as resources. For some of you, you are like Michael, you have no siblings, or parents who paved the way before you. Ask questions of the adults at your school or parents of friends to learn what is possible, and find people who will help you get there.

The truth is that no matter what your background, the college application process will require you to have encouragers, realists, gentle pushers, cheerleaders, and mentors. Find your village of believers and you will thrive.

One final note: now that you have the matter of school in control, let's get to thinking about the endless possibilities of colleges and the secrets you need to make sure you will have plenty of choices.

Final Note:

Now that you have the matter of school in control, let's get to thinking about the endless possibilities of colleges and the secrets you need to make sure you will have plenty of choices.

CHAPTER 2

YOUR PRE-APPLICATION PLAN

TIP #5: There are plenty of colleges in the sea. The trick is to start fishing early.

TALE:

"My name is Justin, I'm a freshman."

"Before we leave, take a look at the list of questions your counselors recommend you ask while we are there." I took on the role of college counselor to my nephew and served as his chaperone to the college fair. We were only ten minutes from his high school campus so I took the time to explain a few things about colleges. I shared the difference between schools with graduate programs versus undergraduate only, public versus private, and gave him a sense of the size of colleges based on the number of students.

Our plan: stay for at least thirty minutes and stop at 8 to10 booths. For a 14-year-old freshman boy, that seemed very doable, and I had confidence he could stay engaged for that amount of time. Justin pointed me in the direction of his gym and I said, "Ok, I'll let you pick your schools or you can follow my list, just remember to begin by introducing yourself."

With the wooden bleachers pushed up against the walls

and the athletic banners hanging from the ceiling, this gym looked like any other I've seen across the country. Eager college representatives had decorated their table with pens, pencils, brochures, and beautiful banners. "Let's find a friendly face and talk to these reps," I encouraged Justin as we began his search and handed him my list. He waved off the list and found his first target, Gettysburg College. We continued down each row, hitting the likes of University of Bridgeport, Elon College, Marist, Lehigh, the US Army, Villanova, Rutgers, and two of the unexpected favorites, Stony Brook University and Wagner College.

Gettysburg and Bridgeport served as his first guinea pigs, but, by the third college, Justin knew exactly what to do, and by the time he spoke with the man from Stony Brook he was confident and firm with his handshake, "Hello my name is Justin, I am a freshman."

TRUTH:

By the time you are a senior, you will likely need to apply to five to twelve colleges. Narrowing down your list from a sea of over 3,000 is not as easy as it may seem. A college fair is the perfect place for a young 14- or 15-year-old to begin showing maturity, responsibility, and independence. As a bonus, there is real value in learning how to interact with adults, hold short but meaningful conversations,

"Selecting a college is one of the biggest and most impactful decisions you will make."

and ask good questions. With everything available on the Internet, fewer and fewer families likely make their way out for an evening at the local high school gym. The benefit here is this, you can get lots of one-on-one time with real college admission officers who are all too eager to talk about their campus, the military, jobs, and culinary arts. As a freshman or sophomore, your job is simply to go fishing. "But why? Colleges are all the same," you wonder? I want you to consider for a moment that selecting a college is one of the biggest and most impactful decisions you will make. It is a relationship you will have (for better or worse) for the rest of your life. If you have not done your research, it is too easy to select a college based on what is popular, prestigious, pretty, or perfect. Selecting a college based on this criteria instead of your own may or may not work out. So make a plan and start fishing early.

Freshmen and Sophomores:

OK, boys and girls, you must dress for success. This is half the battle. I don't mean wearing your Sunday best, but do note that when you look good, you feel good, and when you feel good, you smile. So go wash your face, put on your best shirt, and go shake hands.

Anchor yourself with good questions. The college counseling office will often offer a sort of "cheat" sheet that is emailed or sent home prior to the college fair. My only advice here is you only need a few good open-ended questions. For example, "Tell me about the available majors for someone with an interest in science or writing" versus "Do you have an engineering or journalism major?" Or, "Please share what students love most about campus life" versus "Do you have fraternities and sororities?"

More importantly, you will want to familiarize yourself with the difference between private and public, liberal arts colleges versus universities, and single gender colleges. Understand there are two-year colleges, four-year colleges, technical, culinary, and specialized colleges. If you live in a large state, start exploring there before venturing out farther.

Juniors:

By the time you are a junior, you know what you like, what you are looking for, and with that comes knowing who you are. Narrow your list of colleges and get more specific in your questions. Caution: you are still at least twelve months away from applying to college and eighteen months away from deciding on your new home. A lot can change between now and then, so start making your list, but add variety to keep your options open.

Seniors:

It's senior year. You have done your research, narrowed your list, and you are ready to cast your line. Congratulations, you are actually fishing!

Wait quietly. The waiting can be difficult, but see this as a reflective and peaceful time. Have faith that several fish have been waiting for you.

Hook your fish and bring them in. Collect your acceptances and celebrate!

Keep it or release it? Decide on the fish for you, and release all the rest.

TIP #6: When it comes to standardized testing—take charge, tackle the exam, and own the score you earn.

TALE:
The SAT Whispers In My Ear

As the Griffin family searched for a summer program for their eldest child, they found a highly regarded program in Baltimore which required the SAT test as an entrance exam. Amie would be the only kid in her middle school to voluntarily take the SAT. When the score arrived, Amie did not understand it, but she thought it was a bit low. Two years passed, and in the fall of her sophomore year, she and her classmates took the PSAT. Amie felt ready to master the exam, but when her score arrived she understood that this was not the score she wanted two years henceforth.

As Amie sat in my office she remembered meeting Yvonne while visiting her grandparents, "Ms. Colón, I think Yvonne is known as the 'SAT Whisperer.'" Amie's father had grown up in Pacific Palisades, and, up until recently, the Griffin family spent most Sundays together. The taxing demands of private school, volleyball, soccer, track, and student council made it prohibitive to do almost anything else but homework on the weekends.

A week later, Amie pleaded with her parents to let her work with the SAT Whisperer. This meant allowing Amie to drive herself to school on Fridays, and after practice, Amie would drive to her grandparents home. With their blessing, Amie got to work. The MIT alumna met Amie the following Sunday to review her SAT and PSAT scores, set goals, and make a timeline. Ambitious in her college dreams, Amie and Yvonne set out an 18-month plan with a goal of increasing her score by 500 points.

Every Friday, Amie was up by six in the morning in order to arrive at school by 7:45 a.m. From 3:15 to 5:00 p.m., Amie practiced passing, shooting, heading, dribbling, and trapping the ball on the soccer field. Even as a sophomore, Amie wanted to improve her game, and for an extra fifteen minutes, she asked her coaches to help her develop strength in her kick and endurance on the field. By 5:30 p.m., Amie was in her car and knew Grandma and Grandpa were waiting with dinner for her and Yvonne. Yvonne carefully designed the first two hours of each meeting to stretch and exercise Amie's brain, complete repetitive math drills, become comfortable with math facts and formulas, and build her knowledge through reading in cross-curricular fields while also developing her analytic skills. The final hour always consisted of a timed practice exam in the area of math, reading, writing and language, or essay writing.

The first two months did not yield an improved score in any section of the exam. Amie was not discouraged. Amie plowed ahead and turned down invitations to meet friends for dinner, a movie, or a party on Friday nights. By February, she and Yvonne began to see movement in her score. Yvonne's lessons grew in difficulty as the skills built on each other from one week to the next. The tipping point came by the end of the sixth month, when Amie grew her score by 100 points. From Saturday to Thursday, the SAT whispered in her ear, like a humming bird that wouldn't go away. Every Friday she woke up with determination and a readiness unlike any other day of the week. She was addicted to improving her score, and for the next twelve months she never looked back.

In the spring of her junior year, Amie registered for the SAT. When her score arrived she knew exactly what the numbers represented. That Sunday, Yvonne was invited to the Griffin family dinner. At her seat at the table, Amie left a printed copy of her test scores with one note, "Thank you for 'whispering' in my ear."

One year later, Amie received her acceptance letter to her top choice school. New Haven, Connecticut, would become her new home.

TRUTH:

Unfortunately, the SAT or ACT is a necessary evil part of this process. I realize it can cause tremendous stress on a student, as well as cause many students to doubt their knowledge and lower their self-confidence. More than increasing your score, the takeaway from Amie's tale is this, do not let this exam define you. Repeat after me, "I am in control of this process." Yes, the SAT will whisper in your ear, so do not ignore that little birdie.

As a college admission officer, at the end of each presentation, I would give the statistics of grade point average (GPA) and SAT scores of the admitted class from the year

"One of the evil truths about college admissions is that the more selective it is to earn a spot in college X, Y, or Z, the more popular it becomes, and, as a result, the college receives more and more applications with each year."

prior. "The mid 50 percent range was between 1290 to1370," I would offer. Let me explain what this means. First, it means that 25 percent of the admitted students scored lower than 1290 and 25 percent scored higher than 1370. I recommend looking up this range and/or asking about it for each school for which you are applying. I have two notes of caution. First, you should always use the middle number of this range as a base line score to shoot for. In this scenario, it would be 1330. Second, the reason for cautionary note number one is that the next admitted class will almost certainly have a higher mid 50 percent range. One of the evil truths about college admissions is that the more selective it is to earn a spot in college X, Y, or Z, the more popular it becomes, and, as a result, the college receives more and more applications with each year.

I applaud colleges that have removed standardized tests as a mandatory part of their admission process. Bravo to these colleges for reminding students a one-time exam does not define who they are, nor does it all together predict college success. That said, I do not see the exam being eliminated anytime soon. So, whether you can give fifteen minutes per day or three hours every Friday, take charge, tackle the exam, and own the score you earn.

TIP #7: There is no better way to find the right college for you than to visit as many as you can.

TALE:

Nittany Lions, RITchie Tigers, and Oski Bears, OH My!

To this day I continue to tell the story of Vassar College. It is indeed one of the most beautiful campuses I have ever seen. Matthew Vassar was a self-made man who made his fortune by brewing beer. With no children, he set out to create a college equal to Harvard and Yale—but for women. And with his vision of an elite women's college, the doors were opened to just over 350 women in 1865. Nearly a century later, the prestigious college was offered, like a hand in marriage, to merge with Yale. Decision makers at Vassar turned down the proposal, but instead opened its doors to men in 1969.

When I set out to travel the country and sell the campus of Vassar College, I could name the number of colleges I had visited on one hand, including the two I had attended. I did not understand how important it is to visit colleges until I became a college counselor. As the Director of College Counseling, I traveled every month visiting campuses all over the country. Colleges would group together up to fifty counselors at a time to visit six to ten schools. You know why? Colleges know that the best way to sell their institution is to get you to visit. For example, one of my favorite tours was known as COWS, Counselors Observing Wisconsin Schools. We were a full busload of counselors from around the country, and each day we were escorted from campus to campus. Believe me, this works. I have visited likely one hundred or more colleges, and I can still rattle off my favorites.

What has been most interesting to me are the reasons I fall in love with these institutions of higher learning. They are not the same each time. For some, I love the beauty of the campus, others I love the people I meet, another favorite has the most number of statues in the US—one has a pineapple on top of the roof—and sometimes it is simply the traditions that come with a school that is over 150 years old. You never know what is going to tug at your heartstrings, so get out there and explore, find your potential suitors.

TRUTH:

I'm going to say what parents do not usually want to hear: choosing a college is a gut instinct. Like choosing a boyfriend or girlfriend, you know when you know. Unfortunately, like love, there is not always a mutual attraction. But, with any luck, by the time you are a senior, you will have found a handful of colleges that can make you happy. There is no replacement for actually visiting a college campus. To see the buildings and landscape, to hear the marching band practicing on the field, to speak with real students on campus,

"When you visit a place that you know is not right for you, do not fret. Rather, take comfort in knowing that you are one step closer in finding the one that is."

and to smell and taste the cuisine while visiting the student center is the best way to meet your prospective match. While it may not be possible to traverse the Great Plains, Rocky Mountains, New England, coastal cities, or the southern belle states, do what you can and you will be the better for it. Some of the best tours were ones I randomly took on my way to a farther destination. Even if you cannot take an official tour, if you can get out of the car and walk around for thirty minutes, you can capture the feel of a campus.

Sometimes your gut tells you right away whether this is a school for you or not. But sometimes it takes a few visits to different types of colleges to begin to find the right fit. When you visit a place that you know is not right for you, do not fret. Rather, take comfort in knowing that you are one step closer in finding the one that is.

Recommendations

Before Your Arrival:

1 – Plan Ahead. Go online to the college website, click on

ADMISSIONS, and find the place where you can reserve a spot for an undergraduate admissions tour.

2 – What is a campus tour? The campus tour is typically led by a student ambassador and can last anywhere from 60 to 90 minutes.

3 – Do I also need to attend an information session? An admission officer typically leads an information session and likely reads applications and has a role in making a decision on prospective applicants. If you have time for both a tour and session, do both. If not, choose one and reserve a spot.

Once on Campus:

1 – Arrive early to find parking.

2 – Come prepared with a few questions.

3 – Turn off your phone and keep your eyes open. You will be amazed at what you learn by reading what is posted on bulletin boards, picking up the school newspaper, and watching and listening to students.

4 – Take a few photos. Use the photos to capture something that strikes you and/or will help jog your memory later.

5 – Ask a staff member for the name and email address of the admission officer assigned to your school. If you want to follow up with an email (or handwritten note) it is good to know with whom to address it.

Immediately After Your Visit:

Grab your phone or a college journal and take notes. Spend

five minutes free writing. Write down everything you remember: the good, the bad, and the ugly. Jot down bullet notes, write a paragraph and/or a quick story about the kid you met in the campus center. Draw, doodle, or sketch whatever comes to mind. Just be sure to journal something within a couple of hours after leaving.

TIP #8: Show up on TIME. Keep TRACK of Your Accomplishments. Say THANK YOU.

TALE:

High School: Your Job Interview For College

Several colleges out there have an added space for applicants to answer some obscure question that is only for that particular college. At Vassar ours was called "My Space." It was literally a blank sheet of paper where you could do, write, draw, paint, and submit just about anything. Some of the ones worth keeping include a single shoe delivered with the message, "Now I've got one foot in the door." Another student created a self-portrait of himself made entirely of jelly beans, and one of my personal favorites was a children's book authored and illustrated by the applicant.

As fun as it was to discover each student's "My space," when asked about that portion of the application, I instead turned my focus to what I believe are the three key habits to ensuring that three important parts of your application (transcript, resume, and letters of recommendation) are as stellar as possible. Let me put it this way, while in high school, you are on a three or three and a half year interview. Spending hours, days, or weeks on that one obscure question or constructing a scale model of the walkway over the Hudson is not going to earn you the big envelope alone. The transcript, resume, and letters of recommendations are items that will evolve over time and cannot be ideally created or invented at the last minute. Here are the three key habits to develop based on my experience as a college admission officer and college counselor.

Show up on TIME:

Nayeli, "Naya," lived thirty-five miles from school, which can be hours on the freeway in Southern California. She and her father, Mr. Nuñez, left the house at 6 a.m. every morning. While not completely practical to live so far away from school, the Nuñez family lived in Long Beach for its accessibility to the metro, walkable neighborhoods, trendy restaurants, and nearby ocean. A huge proponent of utilizing mass transportation, Naya's father had taught her how to navigate the city via trains and buses. On the rare occasion that Mr. Nuñez had a meeting near home, Naya was able to get to school on her own and was never once late to class. Nayeli loved school, loved her teachers, and used her time after school to get involved in everything while waiting for Dad to pick her up and take the two-hour drive home. Naya spent time in teachers' classrooms practicing her Model United Nations competition speeches, writing for the literary magazine, and building robots with her friends in the science lab. Naya was a favorite among her teachers, but not just because she was likeable, it was the respect she showed for education.   While some peers who lived twenty minutes from school showed up ten minutes late to class, latte in hand, Naya would never think to walk in and interrupt a teacher's classroom. More than this, Nayeli knew that missing a quiz or part of a test would result in coming to class at lunch or after school, and she had far too many friends and activities to catch up with. For Naya, it simply was not worth the trouble of being late, so she vowed to always be on time.

Keep TRACK of Accomplishments:

Raised by a single mom, Ignacio "Nacho" Gonzales thrived since he could walk. Nacho sang, danced, played the piano and electric keyboard, but that is what he did for fun. In an attempt to find Nacho's talents, mom enrolled him in all the typical and atypical sports and hobbies. Ms. Gonzales found her son enjoying sushi by the age of three, excelling in karate at a rapid speed, and drawn to the vibrant colors of anime. His dedication to the art of karate had earned him a junior black belt by the time he was fourteen years old. It was no surprise that Nacho worked as an assistant to his Sensei while continuing to hone his craft and earn his black belt in high school. As a junior, he led the art club, won local and regional awards for his anime drawings, and had shone his work all over Southern California.

Though difficult to keep track of all of Nacho's achievements, his mother recorded everything, just as she had when he was a child. The large plastic purple file box held every award Nacho had received since earning his white belt. Every

June and December, without fail, Nacho sat with his mother and recorded his honors. The printed document affixed to the refrigerator served as fuel to push forward, do more, and get better.

Say THANK You:

Niko grew up in a large home: two parents, and three siblings, each with their own room. Niko's parents lived a very different life as children, having grown up in the Midwestern town of Kokomo, Indiana. With grandparents as farm owners and union workers, Niko's parents went out of their way to inspire the notion of imagination and reading instead of the perfunctory teenage pastimes, such as, television, video and computer games, or movie watching. Niko much preferred setting up obstacle courses in the backyard, tinkering with cars, or inventing science experiments. As a result, Niko was addicted to "how-to" videos found on the Internet and developed an unquenchable thirst for knowledge. He came prepared for class each day and peppered his teachers with questions that often began with "why." While some teachers might become frustrated with the constant inquisition, Niko's genuine interest showed through, and that is what made it special. Niko's questions spurred new conversations and discussions in the classroom, often taking the topic to a deeper level. Teachers loved it.

As he exited the classroom, a simple, "Thanks, Mr. Cendejas," or "Great lecture Dr. Edwards," melted off his lips, and his eyes beamed with excitement.

TRUTH:

Believe it or not, the counselor and teachers are very honest in those letters of recommendation, and before you know it you will need to

"A teacher has the ability to paint the picture of who you are as a person in a few words."

ask them to become your advocate for college. As effusive as they are with lauding your accomplishments in the classroom and leadership in the community, a teacher has the ability to paint the picture of who you are as a person in a few words. Hear me when I tell you that they want nothing more than for you to succeed. By showing up on time and keeping track of your accolades, you will have plenty of material to give your teacher to write about— this is half the battle. It is the appreciation you offer at the end of class and the genuine interest you show in class that will speak volumes.

I used to give teachers a tip of ending a letter in one of a few ways: "Calyn is the best student in period 5," or "Josh is the best student I have taught this year," or "Montana is one of the best writers I have seen in the last five years," or "Brandon is by far one of my best students in my twenty year career." Using this one sentence at the beginning or end of a letter, a teacher has clearly given us the information we need. And there are several adjectives that you can use here: best leader, kindest student, most compassionate, best debater, the

"With each day in high school, you have an opportunity to create and design who you are to the world."

hardest working, etc.

The truth is, you have a clear strength as a student and as a contributor to your community. Whatever it is, be the best at it. With each day in high school, you have an opportunity to design and create who you are to the world. If you have a habit of being late, no problem; commit to being on time for the next thirty days, and it will become a habit. If you are a sophomore and have yet to get involved on campus, no worries; there are plenty of organizations that have been waiting for you to join, so get moving. And if you have never thought about thanking your teachers, it is the best gift you can give to any and all of them. A simple, "Thank you," on your way out the door will go a long way. Trust me, s/he will notice.

Final Note:

Add to your to-do list: Learn about colleges. Start studying for the SAT. Visit different types of colleges. Be on time. Keep track of activities. Say thank you. These key habits will get you off to a great start in controlling your own destiny in the college admission process. Remember, 90 percent of your application happens well before senior year. Don't put off tomorrow what you can do today. You control this process.

Next step: fill your resume.

CHAPTER 3

YOUR RESUME PLAN

TIP #9: Get off your phone and look up! Join a club and meet new friends in person.

TALE:
Something To Talk About

Once in a while, an applicant comes across as seemingly "perfect." There is Brenda who wants to become a nurse, has spent the last two years volunteering at the local hospital, earns extra spending money by babysitting, and completed her Gold Award for Girl Scouts by making and collecting warm blankets for newborn babies. Or Jorge who has played soccer since he was three years old, is now the captain of his school and club team, has collected cleats and uniforms each year to deliver to young players in Mexico, leads the Future Business Leaders of America club, and wants to major in business with an emphasis in sports management. WOW. Impressive.

If you are in middle school or a freshman in high school, this should not sound familiar. These "perfect" (no such thing) applicants did not happen overnight. Every student goes through a process of figuring out the answer to the following questions: Who? What? When? How? and Why? (WWWHW). Who do you want to spend time with? What do you enjoy? When do you have time in your day? How can you contribute your talents? Why is this important to you?

Just like your grades and test scores tell the story of what admission officers often call your "AQs," Academic Qualities, your co-curricular resume will describe for the reader your "PQs," Personal Qualities. At the risk of making it sound as though your academic profile is less important, I want to remind you that every single applicant comes to the table with a grade point average and a test score. For now, let's assume everyone begins on equal footing with regards to AQs.

As your college counselor, I suggest you begin developing your resume sooner rather than later. For some students, their entire resume is filled with performing arts: plays, dance, and acting competitions. A similar student might enjoy performing arts as well but only participates in the fall because her primary contribution is on the robotics team, which competes in the spring. For students who most enjoy spending their time on the field or on the court, they might contribute their hidden talent by singing in the church choir. Emerging leaders may discover a passion for speaking and hone that craft by joining the Speech and Debate Team or by becoming a school ambassador. There is no perfect pathway to college. There is also nobody else like you. You are unique, and the possibilities are endless on what to do and how to immerse yourself in the joy of school.

If joining new clubs and meeting new friends is hard for you, rest assured you are not alone. Why not invite a classmate to join you at the club lunch meeting? Or better yet, ask Mom or Dad to bake or buy some cookies to bring to the meeting, and you are sure to be a hit with others. The longer you wait to join a club, try out for a team, and explore new activities, the easier it will become to stay glued to your smart phone and video games. That may suit you now, but once you are applying to college, you will have nothing to talk about and risk the chance of having the AQs, but all too few PQs.

Your only job in life right now is to go to school. So why not make it fun, try new adventures, hone a skill, and get out of your comfort zone? Adults today believe that there are way too many students attached to their phones, computers, and video games; and as a result their heads are staring at a screen instead of looking up and out into the world around them. Push yourself to embrace high school, because one day you will wish you were a kid again.

Get out there and give us all something to talk about!

TRUTH:

With each application, I had a form to jot down notes: things that stood out, questions I had, and academic and personal highlights of each candidate. There was a spot for any student who held a key leadership position, such as Student Body President, Editor in Chief, Captain, Gold Award, or Eagle Scout. This spot was also reserved for the even more rare awards like a regional or national champion, which could range from sports, science fairs, or visual or performing arts competitions. For most applicants, that spot was left blank. On a typical day of reading, I captured the most

"When you become interested in life around you, you become a more interesting applicant."

impressive activities and adventures of the applicant. I noted the personal essay topics and the personality that came through. I highlighted how the counselor and teachers described a student's contributions in and out of the classroom. Reading an application was exciting to me; it was like taking a tour of the student's life and dissecting who he is or what she is most proud of.

On occasion, I would breeze through an application much more quickly than others. I closed the red file and thought, "Did I miss something?" Invariably, the answer was no. Unfortunately, there was not much to talk about in the file.

What you do outside the classroom says as much as, if not more than, what you do in the classroom. Go on, get up and discover the answers to Who? What? When? How? and Why? When you become interested in life around you, you become a more interesting applicant and have plenty to talk about!

Here are a few recommendations for building your resume:

Freshmen, your high school may overwhelm you with the number of opportunities offered. Take time to look around, meet new people, and try a number of activities, clubs, arts, and sports. ADVICE: Join, run, lead, spike, pitch, defend, act, paint, or dance; just don't let this year pass without doing something.

Sophomores, it is early enough in your high school career to take advantage of the missed opportunities from last year. Do anything you wished you had done before; whether you end up loving it or not, you will be sure not to have any regrets. ADVICE: Walk through new doors and create new opportunities.

Juniors, you are entering a very challenging year of high school. What makes this year tough is that the reality of your efforts (or lack thereof) is made crystal clear when you apply to college. ADVICE: Don't wait any longer to discover your WWWHW. Don't wait to become a leader, go out and break personal records and/or sing your heart out on stage. By the end of this year, you will want to make sure you have plenty to talk about.

Seniors, you have approximately 300 days left with your classmates. This year will be packed and busy, but be sure to spend quality time with friends. ADVICE: Have faith that your future is bright. Create lasting memories with every adventure, competition, performance, game, and service and leadership opportunity.

TIP #10: There is no right way to do community service, only your way.

TALE:
How We Serve-ice Our Communities

The very act of doing something with no expectation of getting something in return can fill your soul. Your act may be as simple as helping during a Thanksgiving food drive, donating your artistic skills to design the poster for the school musical, or giving up buying a daily beverage for a week to make a financial donation towards the senior class gift. What most high school students fail to grasp is that there is no "right" way to do service. When it comes to considering how you might serve your community, bear in mind that you have three options. You can give your time, your talent, or your treasure, each of them is equally important.

While recruiting for Vassar College, I was often asked about community service. Over time, I came up with three examples to share as my answer. Consider the following three students as examples of serving on a local, regional, or national level.

TIME: Kendra grew up in a suburb of Los Angeles. Beginning at the age of 5, her summer was spent at Ballona Beach Cities Day Camp. Shy and nervous at first, with each year that passed, Kendra became more courageous in moving from swimming to paddleboarding, surfing, and kayaking. New campers began to look to Kendra for encouragement and an enthusiastic "You can do it" on the sands of the Pacific Ocean. It was no surprise that Kendra was invited to become a junior counselor, lead songs after the aquatics activities, and help with the "New Bees" at camp. Kendra returned every year selflessly. She did not know what a profound difference she made, and yet she gave up her summer to ensure that campers like Becky, Paul, Mara, Jules, and Malik had an enjoyable time at the best beach camp in town.

TALENT: Roy was always a mover and a shaker from Seattle, Washington. I never understood how Roy could get students to give up a Saturday to clean National Parks, build houses, or tutor middle school students, but he did. He delivered a message that tugged at your heartstrings, and before you knew it, you were sucked in. Roy's mother was a phlebotomist, and so each year he led the Red Cross Blood Drive. There were plenty of students and teachers who qualified as potential donors. One by one, Roy made the rounds at lunch, "What would you do if you could save three lives in just 20 minutes?" Intrigued by the question that never failed to engage others, Roy would spend the next seven minutes convincing everyone at that lunch table to sign up to give blood. But signing up did not always translate to showing up. Three days before the blood drive, he sent a mass email reminder. The evening before, Roy sent individual texts messages. And the morning of your donation, a mass blind text was sent as a reminder and thank you. Each year the number of donors increased, and the Red Cross recognized him for his efforts.

TREASURE: In November of Kelby's freshman year, she and her family volunteered at "Feed my Sheep" on Thanksgiving morning. Kelby was inspired by the diversity of people who came together to serve and be served. People of all races, age, religious and socio-economic backgrounds from all over Delaware County were in one place to celebrate life and give thanks. Over the course of the next few weeks, she overheard her parents talking with community leaders who said they wanted to expand the operation to serve the number of people in need. Just before winter break, Kelby headed to her art class to finally collect her items that were recently fired in the kiln. She had made a set of four bowls for her family—each slightly larger in size—for her sister, herself, mom, and dad. Walking home that day, a light bulb went off. "Shepherding through Soup" was born. Every fall, all of the bowls produced by Muncie Central High School students go on sale and serve as an entrance ticket for the bottomless soup event held in the school cafeteria. After her first year, Kelby partnered with cross-town rival, Delta High School, and increased the funds raised by 125 percent.

When you think back on a time when you have given your time, talents, or treasure to a worthy cause, you cannot help but smile. Your daily, weekly, or annual deposit, no matter how small or large, will impact others, and that is how you serve-ice your community.

TRUTH:

There are hundreds of ways in which we can serve our local, regional, national, and/or global community. When you discover your gifts, embrace them, and then utilize them to change our world in whatever capacity you can. There is no right way to serve, only your way.

"College campuses everywhere need leaders, coordinators, motivators, movers and shakers, as well as, altruistic do-gooders. Stay true to who you are and service your community!"

When I first began working in college admissions, I admit, I did not get it. I did not understand that students, parents, and counselors alike were looking for the magic formula. "Tell me what to do and I'll do it." They wanted answers to how to get in, what to do, and which particular activities should be attached to the resume. Service seemed to be all the rage back then and still is. I read hundreds of applications of time spent with underprivileged kids, building homes, serving in local soup kitchens, and food and clothing drives.

The truth is this: giving back is one of the greatest life lessons we can learn when we are young. I want to encourage you to find a way to give your time, talent, or treasure. If literally serving soup or reading books to youngsters is not your calling, I promise you, this is perfectly fine. College campuses everywhere need leaders, coordinators, motivators, movers and shakers, as well as, altruistic do-gooders. Stay true to who you are and serve-ice your community!

TIP #11: If you join a team just for a winning record, you are in it for the wrong reasons.

TALE:
Habits of a Team

A student of the game, Coach Mitch had turned down an athletic scholarship to play at a small college to instead become the team manager for a successful Division I college team in the Midwest. Bringing his knowledge to the Viking team that year, Coach Mitch and the team hobbled through the end of the season with mixed success. By the end of the year, some families chose to transfer in search of a school with a winning program. Coach Mitch wished them well, "Dr. Colón and I will always welcome you back home."

His plan was simple: get the boys on a solid and consistent training and eating plan, methodically practice and master the basic skills of basketball, and play against the best competition possible, as often as possible. Each day practice was a grind: footwork, dribbling, passing, shooting, and rebounds. A few more students gave up, but most stuck with the program as they gradually noticed personal improvement. With early success in pre-season, the team made a commitment to Coach Mitch and did exactly what he said. They won and won often. This was great, except it was time to reorganize the teams in our league, and our recent success meant our competitor schools voted our team to move up to the next league. This would not be good for winning. When I delivered the news to Coach Mitch, I was startled by his reaction, "That is the best news I've heard all year. Great!"

In his second full year as head coach, Mitch led with enthusiasm at every workout, practice, and every game. His quest to win was nothing short of preparing for a David versus Goliath battle. This was like being the best AAA baseball team and then moving up to play against all the top major league teams the following year. We had 1000-1 odds, but Coach Mitch understood that playing against the best only made his team hungrier. Coach repeated his philosophy of consistency of actions leading to excellent habits. The team had tasted success in the summer and now bought into the idea that winning was a short-term goal, but consistent improvement would prevail. He believed in his boys and so they followed.

That season, the Varsity Viking Basketball team went from failure to failure with absolute enthusiasm. They lost every single game with the exception of one near the end of the season. At the end of the season, Coach explained that the strength of our league teed us up to receive a birth in post-season play. Moved to compete against a more appropriate group of schools, play-off games began. Two weeks later, we won the coin toss for the location of the semi-final game against the number 1 seed. The gym was packed, and the game came down to the final seconds, and we landed victorious. With one game left, the California Interscholastic Federation (CIF) Championship title was within our grasp.

The reigning champs were not prepared for our team. Our Vikings stayed on them for thirty-two minutes, a habit not formed overnight but over time. Their hard and fast play was evident, only achieved by practicing the habit of quick thinking, watching everywhere, and relying on teammates to be there. The Vikings ball skills had been honed by repetition of shooting the ball correctly every single day. And their fierce commitment to rebounds only proved their commitment to win. At the end of the thirty-two minutes, the unlikely winner proved to everyone that natural talent can only take you so far, but when honed, with repetition and commitment, talent can be transformed into the habit of excellence. It is the habit of excellence that wins championships. Bravo, Vikings!

TRUTH:

There are a multitude of lessons woven in this tale: quitting is not an option, transferring is not the answer, failure is a good thing, and, with consistency, excellent habits are formed. If you can join a team sport in high school, do it. Even if you are not the best player on the team, even if you sit on the bench more than you play, do it. The life

"The life lessons of failure, team, success, and hard work are served up best in a team sport."

75

lessons of failure, team, success, and hard work are served up best in a team sport.

Over the last decade or two, there has been a movement of more and more high school aged students joining club team sports. Whether it is travel ball for baseball or softball, club volleyball, or private weekend tournaments for basketball, thousands of high school athletes have decided to try and master one sport in lieu of attempting several. This has altered the landscape of high school athletics. The would-be football, basketball, and baseball player now only participates in winter basketball. The would-be volleyball, soccer, and softball player now only participates with her club volleyball team year-round in hopes of receiving a college scholarship. While this is a family decision, and you will choose what is best for your son or daughter, please hear me out:

1 – When students are engaged with their peers, teachers, and coaches, they feel more connected and happier at school.

2 – Even if you choose to participate outside of school, give your talents to your own high school as well.

3 – Receiving a full or partial athletic scholarship is tough, be sure to never take your eyes off the real prize: academics.

4 – Whatever you choose, whether you are winning or failing, be sure you never lose your joy and enthusiasm!

TIP #12: You are best served by also building a resume off the field.

TALE:

When Opportunity Knocks, Seize It. Carpe Diem!

"Dr. Colón, we want to invite St. Bernard as one of three schools to participate for one year. Can you select six sophomores who you see as potential leaders?" This was an honor from Loyola Marymount University, LMU, and the obvious answer was, "Of course, I'll have the list ready for you by next Friday." I smiled as Darin and I shook hands. I called in the Assistant Principals, "How are we going to choose?" The six students would miss a half-day for the next 10 months.

We nominated five girls and five boys and sent out 10 letters to the parents and selected students. Knowing that some of the dates conflicted with after school activities, we were sure that not every family would agree.

Stephen's mom was the first one to call and come into the office. We spoke at length as I discussed the curriculum of the program and the opportunity for her son. When looking at the ten dates, baseball would prove to be a conflict for Stephen. Mrs.

Moreno secretly wanted Stephen to say "yes," but she would allow her son to arrive at his own decision.

That evening, Mr. and Mrs. Moreno had a family meeting to explain the full opportunity to their son. Stephen listened but was unsure of what to do.

Stephen arrived early the next morning in full dress uniform, his navy school tie hung down his chest as he walked into Coach Alvarez's classroom. Coach read Stephen's nomination letter and congratulated his pitching protégé. Coach Alvarez had pitched for the major leagues for a brief period and had taken a liking to Stephen's pitching style. They spoke about the pros and cons, about Stephen being very late to practices, and missing one or two games. Coach never gave Stephen his answer but instead gave him questions that he should answer and sent him off with two little words on a sheet of paper.

"What does this mean, Coach?"

"When you find out, you'll know what to do."

The very next morning, Stephen accepted his nomination and filled the sixth spot.

Once per month, the LMU High School Academy cohort of six waited to be picked up by noon and then made two more pick ups for a total of 18 students from three high schools. Mrs. Moreno would report with great pride on each session, "They lunched in the 'such and such' fancy dining space and listened to 'so and so' prominent speakers. Stephen enjoyed practicing his interview and thinks he might have an internship this summer."

In February I checked in with Coach Alvarez about

Stephen's tardiness to a few practices. He assured me it had not been a problem, "Actually, when he is there I notice that he takes the initiative to get the boys organized, gets out the equipment, and leads the team in prepping the field." Ironically, Stephen was rising as a leader among his 18-member cohort at LMU as well.

At the end of the eighth session in April, each of the members of the LMU Academy was given a special offer. LMU had decided that rather than exchange this group of 18 for a new crop next year, they wanted to see this same set of students through the end of their senior year and include college counseling and SAT preparation. This was a one-time offer to continue with the Academy for two additional years.

It was no surprise that Stephen had kept that piece of paper with two little words from Coach Alvarez tucked away on a shelf in his room. He had already said "Yes" to two more years, and for further encouragement Stephen read the words again, "Carpe Diem."

TRUTH:

Stephen, his coach, and his parents did not begin this journey with LMU knowing that it would lead to three years of advice, role modeling, and skill building. They all believed this opportunity was for one year only, and look what happened. Stephen's desire to continue with the program and his network of support, led to an amazing

"Your application must also impress the group of college admission officers, not just the coach."

journey of personal growth. As a senior, Stephen maintained a 3.8 grade point average, led his cohort members at LMU, joined the first robotics team to compete for St. Bernard, became a Campus Ministry leader, and was voted by his teammates as captain of the baseball team. Stephen became the leader he was meant to be for his peers, his school, and the communities of which he is a member.

Stephen now has a full resume as he applies to colleges. His participation in the Academy, a variety of activities, and his growth as a leader make him a much more attractive applicant. With all of his acquired skills, Stephen also knows how to impress the coaches he meets. The key is to make a coach's "list" of recruits. The system I learned was such that the coaches turned in their A, B, and C lists. The lists from the coaches differed by degree of talent each student had and therefore desirability for a spot on the team was denoted as, "A, B, or C." As a Division III institution, we often admitted a speckled group from among all three lists, not just the A list. Why is that important to you? Think about it: your application must also impress the group of college admission officers, not just the coach. Ultimately, it is the admissions office that makes the call. In this case, Stephen will rise more easily to the top of the crop, no matter his recruit level in baseball.

Opportunities do not always present themselves, but when they do, *carpe diem!*

NOTE: Division I recruiting is a whole other ball game. (pun intended)

TIP #13: What you do becomes your resume. Why you do it becomes your college essay.

TALE:

School: A Home Away From Home

Josiah was the quintessential "Mr. Everything." Being good at nearly everything wasn't always that easy. Never quite big enough or fast enough for football, instead he tried out for the tennis team. He sang well enough, but was much better on stage, memorizing lines and delivering them with heart. Though well-known throughout many different cliques on campus, Josiah purposely chose the safer route and was elected by his classmates for Class Council instead of running for Student Council. By the time he was a senior, Josiah was Senior Class Vice-President, captain of the tennis team, actor, robotics and Key Club leader, and Josiah even led the church youth group on weekends. To the outside world, he led a charmed and fulfilling life.

Josiah's close friends, Cyndie, Jess, and Larry knew the truth. Josiah actively avoided his home as much as possible and found love at school. The enormous amount of hours he spent on campus was equally less and accident as more a strategic plan to spend as few hours at home as possible. The early part of the fall brought the opportunity to take his frustrations out on those yellow-green tennis balls, swinging back and forth across the net. Early October was filled with rehearsals, cast gatherings, and an excuse to help with the stage sets on weekends. Josiah found his people in theatre more than any other organization. He found friends who were odd yet quirky, smart yet awkward, joyful yet sad, strong yet weak, and each was driven, ambitious, and hard-working in the face of some adversity in his or her life.

Robotics, Key Club, and Class Council kept Josiah busy throughout the year, and especially in the spring, but it was the theatre that kept him physically on campus. Even when meetings and robot sessions ended at 8 p.m., Josiah could always find Mrs. Kofenya working with actors or Mr. Hartigan using power tools with the student crew. Like a father teaches his son how to change a tire or swing a bat, so too would Mr. Hartigan teach Josiah a new skill with the jigsaw power tool. Josiah was grateful and took those new talents with him to the robotics build team. When the robotics team competed in the annual FIRST competition in the spring of his junior year, Josiah invited Mr. Hartigan to come watch and support the team. Mr. Hartigan obliged and happily wore his safety glasses to be on the floor with the team. Josiah beamed as his mentor assisted with twisting and tweaking of a few pieces on the team robot.

One fall afternoon on a Saturday, Josiah put down the power saw and asked, "Mr. Hartigan, I would be honored if you would become an honorary member of Team Record-Sea-Ker as a coach." Mr. Hartigan was well aware that many of the students' parents volunteered nights and weekends throughout the competition season, but with a father who worked night shifts and a mother who was often missing in action, for Josiah, that was not an option. Mr. Hartigan stopped dead in his tracks, walked towards Josiah, and reached out for a hug, "No, son, it would be my honor."

TRUTH:

Josiah added to his resume year after year by spending as many as 10 – 15 hours per day on campus. He literally filled his "dance card" with nearly every club, organization, and performing arts event. What he did in four years became an elongated resume. Good for him. The truth, however, is that Josiah actively avoided his home life and searched for comfort, encouragement, praise, and support from the peers, advisors, and mentors he found at school.

For students like Josiah, it will serve them well to share some details of home life with a counselor and later with the college admission office. Being honest about the stress and strains of Josiah's home life helped in offering context for

"The most impressive resumes are not always the longest. It is the student who can honestly reflect on why s/he chose a group, an organization, and a longtime commitment that will prove most meaningful in the college admission process."

his life and the reasons why he is so involved and determined at school. With a conversation with his counselor, together they can decide how to reveal this information in his application. It could be through his personal essay, but it could also come from the letter of recommendation of his counselor and/or teacher. A good counselor will encourage candor and honesty without pushing the student beyond their comfort zone.

The most impressive resumes are not always the longest. It is the student who can honestly reflect on why s/he chose a group, an organization, and a longtime commitment that will prove most meaningful in the college admission process.

Final Note:

As freshmen and sophomores, continue developing your resume while trying new clubs, community service, sports, outside opportunities, performing arts, etc. Once you have a handle on what you love, as a junior, begin to reflect on why you love it. For some of you it may be obvious: your love of robotics, basketball, or tutoring young kids. But you might be a student for whom the choice you make to get involved is more emotional or personal. It may be that a family member is a cancer survivor and that is your cause, or like Josiah, you escape home by becoming attached to people at school. Why you do anything matters to college admission officers because it matters to you. Involvement shows connection to team, people, causes, interests, and self. Interested students make for interesting applicants. The next chapter will offer examples of students who have developed a compelling "why," be it on accident or on purpose.

Keep up the great work. You are taking control and making magic happen. I am so proud of how far you've come already.

CHAPTER 4

YOUR LEADERSHIP PLAN

TIP #14: Leadership Doesn't Always Come in a Title.

TALE:
When The Going Gets Tough, The Tough Don't Get Going!

Staring out the library window, there were only eight players on the football field. Less than two weeks ago, over 35 players showed up for varsity football. With the resignation of the head football coach, the parents of our young men began entertaining the opportunity of completing their high school years at another school. Lured away by the promise of playing time, large financial aid packages, a winning season, and a chance at being recruited to play college ball, students' and families' loyalty faded. But Wayne was not enticed. As Wayne watched his buddies and teammates leave his alma mater, Wayne remained resolute. His decision to remain at St. Bernard made him the sole senior to return as a varsity football member. As I sat there staring out the window, I was sure the news had been relayed to Wayne that Dr. Colón had cancelled varsity football for that season.

With only eight players, it was not clear to anyone that

St. Bernard would even field a junior varsity team. Wayne called his loyal brothers and walked around at freshmen orientation recruiting others to join the JV squad. By the end of the first day of school, there were 29 students at the football meeting, including six seniors. Practice began the next day.

As a new principal, I did not realize our league rules and policies could differ from the California Interscholastic Federation (CIF) handbook. The league by-laws stated that seniors were not allowed to play on the junior varsity team. I made my plea in writing and requested the team be allowed to play no more than two seniors at a time. Later that week, the league voted against our request. No senior would be allowed to play in a league game. That was that. The conversation lasted no more than four minutes, including the time it took to vote. I was angry. Six seniors showed resolve and made a stance that academics and loyalty to school trumped a fleeting promise on the field. As educators, this is what we teach our students: to stand for something bigger than themselves. I was worried Wayne and his teammates would find their efforts futile.

By 3:30 p.m., the six seniors, head coach, and assistant coach gathered in the conference room. Like pulling off a band-aid, the sting was hot and quick. The tears rolled down their young faces, but when I looked at Wayne, I began to shed my own. Ever positive, Coach said, "We're going to need your leadership on the sidelines, helping to coach our underclassmen. We still need you. We still want you. You're a Viking." Without hesitation, Wayne was the first to say, "You got it, Coach! I'm in."

And just like that, all six seniors remained on the team. They rode on the bus, wore their jerseys on the sidelines, carried water to underclassmen, fetched balls, and even called out plays. The October home game became Senior Night. The 7 p.m. start made for the perfect setting for Wayne and his five comrades to shine in the Friday night lights. The Vikings were 6-0, and on this night, they faced their toughest competitor. Senior Night was not just an opportunity for the Viking community to honor these six upstanding young men, but in fact it was the team's biggest game of the season. The mini army of six wore their home team jerseys, khaki bottoms, and matching blue and gold tennis shoes. Wayne led by example, helping to call plays, encouraging players on the sidelines, delegating assistance for more water, more tape, etc. The game lived up to the hype and proved nerve-wracking for a full four quarters. I grinned from ear to ear as I watched Jason give a heated talk to receiver "Lil Tone." Like a drill sergeant, Wayne got in his face and yelled, "Lil Tone, you're losing your fire!" Down by a field goal with less than two minutes to play... A second down, eight yards to go, resulted in a gain of two yards. Eleven boys huddled, and the crowd stood on their feet. The quarterback scrambled, the ball hung in the air, and fell directly into the hands of Lil Tone who ran like the wind. Touchdown! We were now 7-0.

Two weeks later, the Vikings went undefeated and became League Champions. Wayne and his teammates proved once and for all, when the going gets tough, it is indeed the tough that stay, fight, and win!

TRUTH:

One does not become a leader simply because of a title. No. The label is often given once you have proven you are a leader.

> *"One does not become a leader simply because of a title."*

Your peers are more likely to vote for you on Class Council or Student Council because you have humbly served without a title in prior years. You will earn your spot as editor in chief, captain, lead delegate or actor once you have proven your skills and commitment to the said organization.

When Wayne decided to remain a Viking, he was not the captain of the team. Wayne was a student who wanted to have a great senior year. Doesn't every teen want that? Wayne's "why" was simple: do the right thing for team, school, and family. It was Wayne's personal will and loyalty to school that "accidentally" made him a leader for others to look up to.

If you should find yourself in a situation of whether or not to do the right thing, I can guarantee choosing to do the right thing will lead you down a more prosperous path.

TIP #15: Listen to your inner leader. S/he is knocking.

TALE:
Victories Abound When You Stretch Yourself And Take Risks

An enthusiastic and vivacious student, Danise had a bounty of friends and, as a freshman, she said hello to everyone and always thanked her teachers. She played volleyball and basketball. In the classroom, Danise maintained a solid B average but strived to do better. Without fail, Danise met weekly with her counselor, Ms. Maffei, as they went over her grades, a study plan, and weekly assignments. Having lost her mother before the age of 10, Danise enjoyed the patience and loving care Ms. Maffei offered with each visit. That year, Ms. Maffei encouraged Danise to try pole-vaulting because she believed Danise's lean and long legs would be a natural fit for the team. With some cajoling from her beloved counselor and the track coach, Danise agreed, and by the end of that season, she set a new record for the junior varsity team. Victory number one.

That summer, Danise's father paid to enroll his daughter in

a pole vault academy at the neighboring university. Danise's sister dropped her off at the high school in the early morning when the campus was abuzz with summer school students. Just after 8 o'clock, Danise walked across the street to meet her new friends, and in the late afternoon, she made the reverse commute back to campus. I found Danise in the hallway, "Hi Sweetie, can I help you? Ms. Maffei is gone for the summer." "Oh no, thank you, Ms. Colón. My dad won't be here until 4 o'clock so I thought I would read," she responded looking like she wanted company more than just a desk. "Well come on in, I have a couch if you'd like." She hesitated at entering the Dean's office, but decided to come in.

Danise quickly became interested in the posters and logo designs in my office. Having recently completed the Student Council retreat week, sketches for the theme for the year, posters for Spirit Week and the Halloween costume dance consumed the walls. I'm not sure if Danise felt as if she had to "earn her keep" to continue hanging out in my office, but before I knew it, she had documented all of the posters into organized word documents for safekeeping. "You should consider running for Student Council next year, Danise." She paused and then quickly dismissed my suggestion with a shoulder shrug, "Eh, maybe."

That fall, as Spirit Week ended, I ran into Danise and said, "That could be you running Spirit Week next year!" Ms. Maffei enthusiastically agreed and shared with me how meticulous Danise's folders were and how she color-codes her schedule. I could see Danise's wheels spinning, but she was still not convinced of her leadership skills.

Throughout the fall, Danise's visits to my office became more frequent. As she waited for her father, she dressed the Student Council bulletin boards, made posters, or counted money from ticket sales. While putting away the Halloween dance decorations, it was Danise who inquired about the various roles in Student Council, "Does everyone have to give a speech?" The truth was, the position she was considering did require an election speech in front of the entire school.

Five months later, Danise surprised me by turning in her paperwork to run for office. "I thought you would not give a speech?" Danise's cheshire grin almost made me laugh out loud before her reply, "I know, but I think I could do a good job." "Well then, Miss Walters, good luck!" I gave her a strong handshake and off she went. Victory number two.

Ms. Maffei was the first to congratulate Danise when she was victorious in winning the role of Commissioner of Activities. Among other things, Danise would oversee Spirit Week, school dances, and the annual St. Patty's extravaganza. Just like she had done in pole-vaulting, Danise not only completed her job as Activities Commissioner, she set a new standard. Victories three and four.

TRUTH:

I believe there is an inner leader in you right now. I really do. Sometimes you cannot see it or hear it. There are likely friends, teachers, counselors, and even your parents who have pointed out your strengths and suggested ways to offer your gifts to the world.

The challenge is to listen to that voice, hear their suggestions, and then act on them. Only you can make this choice.

It takes courage to step out of your comfort zone and become vulnerable while standing in front of your peers to give a speech. I know. I get it. But trust me when I tell you that high school just might be the safest place to take that risk. At the end of the day, you will still have your family and friends who love you unconditionally. Plus, the rewards are sweet if in fact you win.

The double bonus in this story is that Danise discovered a belief in herself that proved to be her "why." Once you believe have a greater gift to offer your community, you too will be

> *"The soundtracks you play in your head will help you or hurt you in high school."*

provoked to act on it. The soundtracks you play in your head will help you or hurt you in high school. If you continue to say or think, "I can't," then you likely won't. On the other hand, when your soundtrack is positive and encouraging, you can conquer the world. It took a village of supporters for Danise to finally decide on her own to run for office. Consider this: Who is currently supporting you and pushing you to become the leader you've always dreamed of? Are you listening? Count me as one of your biggest fans, and I'm telling you, "You can do it!"

TIP #16: Change begins when students are fueled into action. Allow your passions to guide you.

TALE:
Take A Stand, Take Action, And Take On The World

Regina walked into the office teary eyed, and her best friend, Annie, was there to explain. On the round lunch table, Regina and Annie saw the "N" word boldly written across Regina's notebook. Regina told Ms. Reynolds that she felt badly because she made the freshman volleyball team and so many others had not. Distraught, Ms. Reynolds tried to console, "You are kind, Regina, but that is no reason for anyone to use that word. I will need to let Ms. Colón know what happened."

By the end of the day, nearly everyone on the girls JV and varsity volleyball team knew of the incident and were appalled that a freshman had the audacity to use that word. The school community had survived an "N" word incident just six months prior in the spring semester. Just when wounds were healing, the students of color would feel demoralized yet again.

Cathy Oh, President of the newly founded Diversity Club, spent most of her time at lunch listening to students. The minority students felt unwelcomed and uncomfortable on campus, while the Caucasian students tiptoed around their peers, not knowing what to say or what not to say. A deep chasm was growing by the day and there was palpable tension in the air.

One afternoon, Cathy came to me with her idea to make a movie. She suggested a sort of documentary, interviewing a cross section of students from all grade levels and all backgrounds. At the next Diversity Club meeting, Cathy gave the members a sheet of paper with10 questions to answer. The key for Cathy was to not make this movie about race, but to be inclusive of the "Big 8," including, race, religion, socio-economic status, ability/disability, ethnicity, age, gender, and sexual orientation. The top five questions that elicited the most candid answers made the short list. Below are those questions.

1 – How do you feel when you enter campus each day?

2 – How is your home life, place of worship, neighborhood, role models – different or the same from what you see at school?

3 – What does the school do really well to make you feel at home, comfortable, welcomed?

4 – What could the school do better to make you feel at home, comfortable, welcomed?

5 – Is there an incident/ event you would like to share about your time on campus? – a positive interaction with a teacher or student or maybe an incident that evoked a sense of feeling like

an outsider.

With a team in place, Cathy spent most of January and February directing her film. As the quiet observer, I witnessed interviewees open up about being on financial aid, taking the public bus for two hours, feeling different due to her religious practices, being outspoken in class about conservative political views and feeling like the minority, being embarrassed each time she needed extended time for a test, having to go home and act as interpreter for her parents, or the international student who entered as a freshman speaking very little English and now was proud of earning her spot in AP English. Then there were the talks of the two "N" word incidents. Students of all backgrounds had an opinion. Some were angry or disillusioned and several were apathetic. After the filming was over, Cathy, often stayed to talk with each student. "Before change can be made, we need to understand where we are and how we got here as a community." Cathy instilled in each one that they were part of the solution and genuinely thanked them.

One month later, the entire student body gathered in the auditorium for the Diversity Assembly. It was a video that needed no introduction. Lights out, film rolled, and the audience went silent. There was plenty to smile about as Cathy had strategically placed much of the positive sentiments at the front end. Soon, the reality of the footage became uncomfortable, while others parts were extremely painful. It's important to note that the movie was also a source of pride for many of those who had often felt like the outsider on campus. They felt heard and there was power in that. In short, the movie was a mirror into the reality of the campus culture at the time, and it forced everyone to ask the question, "What action can we take to do better and be better?"

That school year, Cathy could have just stayed silent and angry. Instead, she took a stand, took action, and began a string of events that would begin shifting the culture for years to come.

TRUTH:

What Cathy did was set off a slew of actions that followed over the course of the next five years. This project did not shape Cathy as a leader; it simply brought out the leader inside. As the president of the diversity club, Cathy had found her passion. It was the disconcerting events on her school campus where she found her "why," and that "why" fueled her into action.

I don't have to tell you the importance of diversity on college campuses today. This is not to say that colleges want a

"A leader, driven by passion is a leader for life."

diverse student body just for the sake of saying they have one. NO! A leader like Cathy is thoughtful about her words and savvy about cultural differences. What makes Cathy stand out in the admission process is not her race, but her willingness to engage in tough conversations and her desire to educate, motivate, and cultivate a community that embraces diversity. In short, Cathy is a leader who was not afraid to take action. As a college admission officer, I want her on my campus. A leader driven by passion is a leader for life.

TIP #17: Pair your passion with great purpose and leave your legacy.

TALE:
Rose Colored Glasses

Olivia has always known she wants to become a doctor. As her college counselor, what impressed me was all of her service to the local community with a commitment to vision care for kids. I only happened upon this information by thoroughly reading the parent questionnaire, but oddly, Olivia made no mention of this in her own resume.

"Olivia, tell me a bit more of the eye clinics you've coordinated? Your father wrote about it in the parent questionnaire," I jumped right in. She was surprised that I knew, so I treaded lightly but needed to understand that this was her project and not her father's. I peppered Olivia with questions: what she did to get the doctors to give up their time, who she connected with at Vista Del Mar, how she decided which families and organizations to invite, and ended the conversation with WHY she chose this as her mission.

It turns out Olivia's father, Dr. Carson, was an accomplished eye surgeon. When Olivia was 11 years old, she accompanied her father at USC's local health fair for neighboring families. Dr. Carson's eye center performed screening eye exams for hundreds of visitors that day at the center of campus. "What happens now, Daddy," little Olivia asked, and Dr. Carson explained the exam would detect vision problems and then he would encourage the families to see their doctor for a full eye exam and get prescription for eyeglasses if necessary. "But what if they don't have an eye doctor?" The simple question stumped Dr. Carson, and he replied, "Now that is a very good question, Livy, and I don't think I have a very good answer for you."

For years Olivia continued to escort her father to community events, watch him work, but more than anything, she wanted an answer to her question, "What happens if a child needs glasses but cannot afford them?" In 8th grade Olivia asked her father if she could put a basket in his office for people to donate their old eyeglasses. He agreed but did not know that she went to various offices and did the same. In just one year, she collected over 100 pairs of eyeglasses. Once Dr. Carson recognized her interest, he encouraged her to make a plan, and she later presented in front of eight eye doctors at their home. They agreed that if she, could in fact, coordinate an eye clinic for local families, they would give their time for eye screenings, vision exams, and donate prescription eyeglasses. Six months later, in the spring of her sophomore year, Olivia and the eight eye doctors hosted a small "Rose-Colored Glasses" event at the Home-Safe Child Care Center in West Hollywood. Since that time, Olivia had coordinated four additional clinics, with a pool of 25 eye doctors, worked directly with Vista Del Mar Child and Family Services, and served a running total of well over 800 families.

With a little prodding, Olivia spent twenty minutes describing the clinics with vivid details of her most recent "Rose-Colored Glasses" event held at Vista Del Mar's 18-acre campus. I can still picture the clinic hosted on the peaceful and spacious lawn in the center of Los Angeles: check-in stations manned with a team of high school student volunteers and eye doctors draped in white coats with their mobile eye equipment, while kids of all ethnicities, wearing shorts and colorful socks, waited in line. Her mission was simple: provide eye exams to the youth in Los Angeles, and for those for whom eyeglasses were recommended, she made sure they were provided for free. Olivia's eyes lit up every time she recounted a story about the kids she met, "Frank was just six years old, Diana loves to read, and Michael had lost his confidence in school." Once she seemed to be out of tales, I asked one last question, "WHY doesn't anyone know that you do this, Olivia?" She looked up at me, "Ms. Colón, it's not about that. It's about the kids."

TRUTH:

This tale touches my heart because I am reminded that, no matter your age, YOU can make an impact on one life and/or an entire community.

At the end of the day, it was Olivia's application and credentials that got her admitted in the Early Decision round of one of the top colleges in the country. Though I was not in the room when the committee made their decision, I can only offer my experience to tell you why I believe she received a "big" envelope, even though she had admittedly lower SAT scores than many of her would-be counterparts.

"The question, "What does this student do with their time outside of academics that is interesting, unique, and/or adds complexity to who they are?" always proved to be an easy way to divide the pile."

Olivia realized her authentic "why" early in her life and found a way to put it all together. First, she came from parents who simply instilled the value of giving back to their daughter. Second, Olivia understood from an early age what it meant to utilize her resources and make a difference in an area in which she was passionate. Third, she was laser focused on her ultimate goal of becoming a pediatrician, but she did not lose sight of the communities around her. Fourth, Olivia did not see the world through rose-colored glasses; she understood that great health care was not provided equally for all. She did what she could to close that gap with eye exams and glasses, knowing the potential to change to trajectory of success for a student in school who, otherwise, could not see the front of the classroom.

When I was an admission officer at Vassar, so many of the applicants were "qualified" - top grades, strong recommendations, and high test scores. The question, "What does this student do with their time outside of academics that is interesting, unique, and/or adds complexity to who they are?" always proved to be an easy way to divide the pile.

When you do what is right, find your inner leader, utilize your passion, then you will indeed leave a legacy. This, my friend, is true leadership.

Final Note:

I want to be clear, without being discouraging. Not every student will discover a true passion or leave a legacy by the time they turn 17-years old. This is not a problem. The point of

"Just like interest makes interesting applicants, an authentic "why" gives authenticity to a college application. "

this chapter is to help you take the time to reflect on your own authentic why. So many teenagers are in a rat race collecting certificates of participation like tickets spitting out of a ski ball machine at your local game zone. Do not fall into that trap. Join a club or sports teams because you love it. Sing, dance, build, or serve because it brings you joy. Discovering your authentic reason why you do anything will catapult you to the front of the stack of applications. Just like interest makes interesting applicants, an authentic "why" gives authenticity to a college application. Trust me, authenticity pops off the page and can motivate an admission officer to fight for you.

So now what? High school is not easy. You must always be willing to push yourself to grow and improve. No worries, I've got a plan for that too.

CHAPTER 5

YOUR SELF-IMPROVEMENT PLAN

TIP #18: Your greatest moment often comes from your greatest failure.

TALE:
Making Lemonade Out Of Lemons

Her khaki pleated skirt shifted from side to side as she took her assigned seat in the library. Two hours later, Gemma was one of the last students to exit. "Have a good day, ladies," Mrs. Jones said good-bye to Gemma and the two others. Mrs. Jones took one last sweep around the private stalls and stopped at a curious folded piece of paper left on the back right hand corner of the wooden armed library chair. Mrs. Jones unfolded the paper and realized what it was: a cheat sheet for the final exam in the chair Gemma had just occupied.

At the end of the following day, I invited Gemma to my office with the junior counselor, Ms. Eaton, present. With my standard first question, I began, "Do you know why you are here?" In this case, Gemma answered with a simple, "No." I explained what was found in her chair just one day earlier, showed her the paper without handing it to her, and asked her to tell me about it. I was pleased when Gemma began to explain her situation.

While she did not deny that it was her piece of paper, she did deny using it during the final exam. Tears welled up as she described, "Ms. Colón, the pressure is so much. I have to keep up with basketball and my grades. I have to get into a good college." I stared back at her—into those deep brown eyes, "But Gemma, what I don't understand is that you were doing well in this class." She went into the final exam with an A-, a perfectly acceptable grade. "I know, I don't know why I doubted myself," she claimed it was a security blanket, that even though she knew the material, she wanted to ensure an A on the exam. Unfortunately, from my vantage point, Gemma was about to earn an F on her calculus final, which would move her coveted A- down to at least a straight B.

The next day Gemma returned to hear the "verdict" in a second meeting that now included her parents. Suffice to say everyone was remorseful of the obvious mistake, supportive of Gemma, and ready to accept the consequences. Truth be told, this was not what I was expecting. The pressure of athletics and school that Gemma had described the day before often comes from home; one or both parents that have ingrained into their child's head that nothing less than the best will do. I did not find that in this set of parents, and I was so pleased that their response was to support Gemma while accepting the decision of the school. Their willingness to view this mistake as a stumble, instead of a catastrophe, played a key role in how Gemma would ultimately handle her situation. The verdict included a four-day in house suspension to begin when we returned in January.

As a junior, Gemma could have decided her life was over; however, this scholar athlete was determined to keep moving forward. Part of her four-day suspension was to meet with me for the last 30 minutes of school. I mentored her, and on the third day I planted a seed about starting a peer council, "You know, the principal has always wanted the students to own the discipline process." The next day Gemma came bounding into my office with a binder of researched honor and peer councils from around the country. She became obsessed with creating a peer council for her school. Gemma's proposal to the principal was approved and soon an interim group of 12 students, produced a constitution, voting procedures, and elections by spring of the following year. In her college essay, she recounted her efforts of becoming one of the 12 founders of the peer council. I'm proud to say, Gemma was admitted to her first choice school.

TRUTH:

Resist the notion that you must become the ideal applicant. I read 25-35 admission files per day, and pretty and perfect was sometimes boring. Life is simply not that easy, nor free of challenges along the way. Some of the most interesting essays were those stories where the applicant recounted a stumble, great or small, and their decision to get up, try again, push forward, and not allow the past to determine their future. Once she owned her failure, Gemma

"Resist the notion that you must become the ideal applicant."

was determined to make amends with all of those she disappointed, including herself. Equally important to Gemma was her wish to teach other students that they too should always believe in their own knowledge and not resort to cheating.

Whether her motivation to start the peer council was

"Some of the most interesting essays were those stories where the applicant recounted a stumble, great or small, and their decision to get up, try again, push forward, and not allow the past determine their future."

purely altruistic or not does not matter. What matters here is with nearly zero recovery time, Gemma dusted herself off and found a way to turn her lemons into lemonade. Some students feel embarrassed after even the smallest of mistakes and then shy away from the adults in their life. While others live in denial and pretend it never happened. Neither of these strategies are good ones, nor should you entertain your desire to ignore the situation.

Don't let a stumble get you down, find a way to make lemonade.

TIP #19: Feelings of inadequacy are natural. Don't allow them to hold you back.

TALE:
Like A Blade Of A Sword, Rejection Pierces The Heart

Cyndie stood over the round receptacle tearing the official letter piece by piece in front of the very teacher who had issued that letter. As the bell rang, Mrs. Rosenberg raised her voice just a bit, "Everyone, take your seats." Making her statement known, Cyndie continued tearing her notice until she could not tear anymore. With a flip of her cheer skirt, she walked away from her otherwise front row seat. Cyndie was in no mood to raise her hand in English class. Today was not her day. Kristin knew not to say anything, but in support of her best friend, she too sat at the back of the room for the first time all year.

Kristin and Cyndie became quick friends when they were the only two rising freshmen to make the junior varsity cheer team. Since then, they had been inseparable. Cheer team led to joining the Key Club and later that fall they ran for class council and won. Early in the spring semester, Cyndie took a job as a hostess at the local family-owned restaurant and often left school immediately to make her 4 p.m. shift. Cyndie encouraged Kristin to join the school newspaper and take photos at the after-school events.

Sophomore year, the two continued to conquer the world of high school. In addition to the long hours on campus for co-curricular activities, the two succeeded in honors classes. Kristin tried acting and landed a role in the fall play and spring musical. Cyndie found her niche on the soccer and softball fields. And somehow they always had time for each other before school, at lunch, and on the weekends.

Popping open the tab of her Dr. Pepper, Kristin suggested, "You know, you should apply for the junior staff spot for 'The Blade.' We're going to need new writers for next year." Cyndie opened her mini chocolate donuts and offered one to Kristin, "Yeah, I thought of that, but I'm not a writer." Picking one out of the sleeve, Kristin took a bite of her mini-donut and paused to remind her best friend of the most important fact, "Cyndie, you would finally have a reason to attend all the games to root for Scott instead of pretending you're there with me." Cyndie nearly choked on her not-so-mini donut and, with that, she decided to apply.

Cyndie needed a writing sample and ruffled through old papers to find one. "Ah . . . this is perfect," she thought. One of her favorite assignments came from the unit on Catcher in the Rye. Ms. DeMuro requested students write a short story using the vocabulary words and keep the character, Holden's, style and diction in mind. Cyndie could not have found a better piece to represent her gifts in writing.

A week later, the bell rang signaling the end of first period, and Cyndie found Kristin among the cackles of high school teens.

"I just got my letter five minutes ago," Cyndie's smile shown her big teeth, "but I wanted to wait for you to open it."

"Well, crazy girl, open it!!"

Emblazoned across the top left hand corner of the white envelope were the words "The Blade" in a crimson-colored stamp. The BHS Buccaneer mascot wore maroon and gold with his arms folded across his chest, sharpened blade in hand.

With a quick tear across the top, Cyndie began to read, but within seconds she stopped and folded it back up.

"I didn't get it. Let's go have lunch," Cyndie was terse in her words and began walking away.

"What do you mean? What does it say?" Cyndie kept walking without a word.

"This must be a mistake, let me read it. Cyndie. Please." Kristin poured over every word twice.

"Two slices of pizza, fries, chocolate donuts, and a Dr. Pepper," this was quite a lunch for Cyndie.

"It says you can apply again early next year, and ..." Cyndie interrupted, "Forget it, I'm not good at writing. That's your thing."

They sat in silence sharing donuts and Doritos before Mrs. Rosenberg's class. That week Cyndie's mini-tantrum tainted her otherwise *perfect* reputation, but it made Kristin love her all the more. In solidarity, Kristin joined Cyndie in outwardly pouting for three days in class. By the end of the week Kristin convinced Cyndie to not take her anger out on Mrs. Rosenberg, and, more than that, to stop beating herself up.

That night, Cyndie's dad took the two peas in a pod out for ice cream. "You both amaze me. Between the two of you, you have nearly tried everything at school. I am proud of you."

With two pink spoons in hand, Cyndie and Kristin dug into their polka dot ice-cream cups.

TRUTH:

Rejection is a necessary part of life. The important takeaway from this tale is this— take your time to pout and be mad, but then it is time to get over yourself. You are not the only one who fails, or gets rejected, or did not make the team, or doesn't write perfectly, so stop feeling sorry for yourself. It is important to learn the lesson early in life that you cannot always win everything. Learn to have a good attitude in the face of rejection. These are the best days to go directly to your happy place and make a list on your phone, computer, or on your bedroom wall of all of your accomplishments. Give yourself a gold star for each of them, and I promise you will feel better. If you can learn that trying and failing is part of the journey to your

"If you can learn that trying and failing is part of the journey to your own success, then you won't take the failure so personally."

own success, then you won't take the failure so personally.

Never beat yourself up. Learn the lesson rejection is teaching you. And, when in doubt, eat ice cream!

TIP #20: Lessons off the field will far outlast those learned in one season of play.

TALE:
Fall From Grace

Once Ken finished his test, he requested permission to go to his locker. Seated next to the now empty desk, Craig took front and back photos of Ken's exam with his phone on silent. By the end of the day, five other juniors received Craig's photos. Thursday afternoon, one of those juniors turned herself in for having cheated on her make-up exam that morning.

"But I did not cheat. I completed my own exam, Mr. Dixon," the junior pleaded his case. Craig McGraw was the pride and joy of his family, a football dynasty. His grandfather, father, and uncle had all played as Varsity Vikings and won state titles in three different decades. Craig had made it his mission for Viking football to return to glory.

"But I have seen that the original text came from your phone," Craig could hear the disappointment in Mr. Dixon's voice.

"Mr. Dixon, I swear, I know I made a mistake with the

photos, but I did not cheat on my exam," Craig's face became beet-red, his heart pounding.

Lesson: Cheating is a choice, not a mistake.

Mr. Dixon had been Craig's freshman football coach and knew then he was destined for greatness. He did everything to contain his heartbreak, "McGraw, tell me right now, what is the academic honor code?" Without hesitation, "I will neither give nor receive aid," Craig lowered his head. "I'm sorry, Coach. I was wrong."

Lesson: Do what is right, not what is easy.

Craig waited in the office while Dean Dixon called Mr. McGraw and scheduled time to meet with me in the principal's office the next morning.

The Vikings were scheduled to play Friday night against a team with a winning record and two seniors already recruited to play Division I college football. Early on in the season, Head Coach Biff (nick named for having played at University of Michigan) and Athletic Director, Carlton Ross, knew that a good fight against this team would prove the Vikings were on the rise. This was the game Craig had waited for all year and his entire extended family planned to watch from the bleachers. A Viking team without the star outside linebacker would make it difficult to hold their offense, let alone have a chance of winning.

At six in the evening, Coach Biff and Carlton tapped on my door, and with a nod, they walked in, "What can I do for you, gentlemen?"

"Doc, the whole team is talking about McGraw..." Coach Biff was a bit heated and Carlton jumped in with a different approach.

"This is about the team, the alumni, and the long-term success of Viking football. We simply want you to keep this in mind," Carlton kept it brief and paused.

I probed, "And if a player circulated photos of your secret plays to another team, would you allow him to play at the next game?"

"With all due respect, Doc, that's not the same. Craig says he himself did not cheat on his exam."

"What Coach means is, we don't disagree that he did something wrong. We just believe a suspension can wait until Monday," Carlton's plea offered an alternative to an inevitable scenario.

"Yes, gentlemen, I hear you, and I'll wait to hear directly from Craig in the morning when his father is present. I remind you that lessons on the field are not the only lessons we teach."

Lesson: Success without integrity is failure.

Mr. Dixon arrived early Friday morning and together we agreed on an appropriate plan based on the values of the institution.

I walked out to the lobby and greeted the two men equal in size and stature. "Please, have a seat. I think you know Mr. Dixon," everyone shook hands and nestled into their positions. "Craig, I would like you to begin by sharing in your own words what happened."

Silence hung in the air, "Dr. Colón, I am so sorry. My actions do not represent who I am. I have let down my team, my family, and myself." Craig took a deep breath as he was about to say the most painful words in his life. Mr. McGraw placed his hand on his son's back, "I'm here, I'm proud." Those words gave Craig the courage to continue, "I would like to accept my consequence of a suspension today and take myself out of the game."

Lesson: Your beliefs don't make you a better person, your behavior does.

TRUTH:

One of my favorite high school coaches used to say, "Football is the biggest thing in *your* life, but it is not the biggest thing *in* life." This tale is a good case in point. We all make mistakes, adults included. But

"As a teenager, you might believe you are invincible, unstoppable, and irreplaceable, and while this may be true for you, proceed with caution."

when you fall, the point is to get up, accept consequences, and proceed with integrity. As a teenager, you might believe you are invincible, unstoppable, and irreplaceable; and while this may be true for you, proceed with caution. Understand that not only is it a good thing to fall, but it is encouraged. If you can fall with grace, the life lessons will far outlast those learned in any one season of play.

With regards to college admissions, this is one of those lessons that may never get retold. Craig's athletic prowess would eventually land him a spot on a Division I football team. But I have to believe that it was his humble disposition and character that shown through every time Craig met a new college coach that eventually afforded him multiple offers. After that incident as a junior, Craig became attentive to his studies and had a nearly perfect record (excluding math class) in his junior year. At the young age of 16, Craig had found a way to fall from grace with humility.

TIP #21: Do your thing. Go against the grain!

TALE:
In Search Of A Dream Team

The oversized maroon and gold bow perfectly matched her maroon skirt with gold peek-a-boo pleats. It's game day, and it's going to be a hot one. It is true what they say, "It never rains in Southern California." Rain or shine, May was Lizzie's favorite month. Cheer try-outs, class elections, and annual banquets. She could not wait to see Shanna and Ramona (Mona) in Mr. Duncan's Health class and share her big news.

"OMG, is he really making us do this?" Mona stared at the board and rolled her eyes.

"Yeah, I heard Cyndie drew number #73 last period. She is stuck with twin girls for the week. But I think it's kind of fun," Lizzie giggled and read the board, "Pregnancy and Parenting."

"Take your seats," Mr. Duncan directed the class and Lizzie asked, "Wait, where's Shanna? I have news to share."

The white board was covered in numbers, #1 to #80 in pink and blue markers. Each one denoted a baby girl, a baby boy, or any combination of twins.

"What's your news, Lizzie? Shanna is gonna be late."

Mr. Duncan walked around the room with a brown paper bag. Lizzie dug her hand in there and pulled out a small piece of paper. "#14," She said out loud so Nadia could cross out the number. "This must be my lucky number. There are only 14 spots open on Drill Team next year. I decided to try out with Valerie and April."

"Lizzie, have you lost your mind? You can't do that. Next year is Varsity Song Team. Hello! This is like the 'Dream Team' of all teams. We've been waiting for this since like, for-eva!" Mona pulled her number and drew twin boys. She could barely breathe, but not because of the two egg babies she would have to carry for the next week. Her best friend had lost her mind.

"I know but the song team doesn't compete. Drill Team performs in parades and competitions, and they wear those tall boots, and two-colored gloves. I'm excited." Lizzie squealed, but the disappointment on Mona's face made her doubt her decision.

Twenty minutes into class, Shanna walked in, drew a number, and handed the piece of paper to Nadia who crossed out number 47. Shanna took her seat behind Mona and Lizzie and could feel them talking about her. "Lizzie, I think that's cute that you are trying out for Drill Team, I support you," Shanna offered a smile that a southern mother would give with the added, "Ah, bless your heart."

While there were 14 spots open on Drill Team, there were less than half of that available on the Varsity Song team, and

Shanna knew that one less person trying out was good news for her. The two weeks leading up to Varsity Song try outs, Mona and Shanna spent less and less time with Lizzie. The three stooges had become the Bobbsy twins. Lizzie was quickly losing her status with the "cool kids." Ironically, that is not what bothered Lizzie the most. She and Mona had been friends since fourth grade, and Lizzie was hurt by how quickly Mona unfriended her.

Lizzie made new friends while learning the Drill Team routines. Valerie and April were all too happy to have Lizzie possibly on the team.

As juniors, they had all made their respective teams. Lizzie saw her songleader friends at the games but was rarely invited to weekend events.

For Lizzie, junior year was one of her most memorable. Drill camp, long practices after school, bus rides to parade events, eating Frito bellies at competitions, and hair spray and high buns were her favorites. Amy, April, Carrie, Valerie, Diane, and Shannon were all fabulous and loyal friends. At the end of the year, though Lizzie loved Drill Team, it was her prerogative, and she decided to join Ramona and Shanna on Varsity Song. She never regretted her decision to leave Drill Team, but if she could have done both, she would have. For Lizzie, Drill Team would always be her Dream Team.

TRUTH:

High School is no cakewalk. The band-width needed these days to survive all the social demands is enough to make any teen go nuts. This tale is about your growth as a maturing teenager within the context of the consequences (real or imagined) that you may face once you *"Show courage in the face of discouragement and independence in the face of social dependence."* make a choice different from your peers. Show courage in the face of discouragement and independence in the face of social dependence.

A student like Lizzie is going to stand out, if the story is told well. This is a story that Lizzie could write about in her own personal essay, but this is also the kind of student that teachers and counselors cheer for (no pun intended). If you have done something in high school that pushes you out of your comfort zone and/or go against the grain of your peers, let me be the first to say, "I'm proud of you!" Share your story with your counselor, in case s/he doesn't know, and strategize together the best way to include your courageous tale in your application.

This story may seem trivial to some, but the truth is, most teenagers don't do the "unpopular" thing. You can choose to not care what other teenagers think of you. Admission officers love to root for a kid like this. When shaping a freshman class, colleges do not want all cookie cutter students. Where is the fun in that? Showing off your independence and rogue personality can work in your favor. So I say, do your thing, go against the grain, and discover your dream team!

"When shaping a freshman class, colleges do not want all cookie cutter students."

TIP #22: Trust your instincts and advocate for self.

TALE:
The Tempest in the Garden

I met Mr. Swanson in September at the national college fair in Minnesota. Dressed in khaki pants and a navy golf polo, Mr. Swanson immediately asked about the 9-hole course on campus followed by a question about the Shakespeare Garden. Impressed with his knowledge, I gushed about both, "The Garden is absolutely my favorite spot on campus." A young man joined us as he moved from the Vanderbilt display to Vassar, "This is where Mom went to college," Mr. Swanson shared with his son. I smiled at the six-foot tall teen and continued, "The golf course is open to the public, but students can play a round for $2." Mr. Swanson paused a moment before filling in the silence, "This is my son, Jeremy, he plays golf and soccer." I shook Jeremy's hand before he sauntered off to visit Villanova's table. Mr. Swanson completed an information card, now officially adding Jeremy to our mailing list. Over the course of the year, I received three email messages from Mr. Swanson noting Jeremy's soccer or golf accomplishments, and he never failed to include an academic highlight. At the close of April and all the admit festivities, I prepared for spring travel, which would take me back to the Twin Cities. "Case Studies" was an annual event put on by a collection of six schools for all junior families. Having read four sample college applications, students and parents were paired with two admission officers and given the task of voting on which applicants would be admitted, wait-listed, or denied.

At the end of the evening, Mr. Swanson stopped in to say hello, "I have been wanting to talk to you about . . ." his words lingered in the air when Jeremy interrupted. "Thank you for coming tonight. I found it very informative. This process makes me nervous." Jeremy's name badge denoted him as an Ambassador and just as Mr. Swanson tried to continue our conversation, Jeremy jumped in to ask about the biology and environmental studies majors on campus.

"Jeremy, why don't you tell Cynthia about your sophomore year."

"I will, Dad, but not now."

I continued to pack up my display while in the middle of a family argument.

"Jeremy, now is a good of a time as any."

"I will, I know. Please, Dad. Not now."

Jeremy had been assigned to help me to my car with any display items or boxes. "Is everything OK, Jeremy?" I inquired. "Yes, my father is worried about my dip in grades in spring of sophomore year. But I assure you, my transcript is flawless this year." I thanked him and gave him my business card.

It would be eight months before I heard from Jeremy again, this time through the one vehicle he had to advocate for himself, his college essay.

I wanted to see Shakespeare Garden. That was the only reason I chose the college trip to New York. Sitting on the bench surrounded by the newly bloomed pansies, I was angry. Why wasn't she the one to bring me here? I wanted my mother to be the one to show me her garden she loved so much. Rushing from soccer practice late October I did not make it to the hospital in time. How could she leave me? Why did I argue with her the night before? I had left the house that morning without an "I love you," or even a "Have a good day." And then she was gone. Just like that. No notice. No warning. No more hugs. I would never forgive myself.

I have no recollection of the rest of sophomore year. I was a zombie, going through the motions of school and yet clearly unaware of my surroundings. The sympathetic looks from teachers only made me despise myself even more. I did not deserve their sympathy; I was a terrible son.

Though I could not speak, that spring, I planted pansies, daisies, and marigolds. I carefully followed the geometrical patterns Mom had laid out. Dad and I added a mulberry tree with a bench underneath, just like Mom had described.

That spring I traded in my golf clubs for rakes, forks, and spades. Instead of putting, I found myself pruning the garden; guiding, directing, and shaping. With her garden in tact, there were days I thought she just might return.

Today, I am no longer that Tempest in the Garden. With each year, the garden blooms more fully and vibrantly, as does my soul.

I could not hold back the tears. It all finally made sense. Jeremy's grades had taken a tumble in sophomore year because of the tragic and unexpected death of his mother. Until now, he had not been able to make sense of what happened, much less find the words to advocate for himself.

TRUTH:

This is a story about a dad trying diligently to advocate for his son, and at the same time, this is a tale about Marco *"Almost every teenager has something that feels like a barrier to success."* coming into his own, making peace with his life's challenges, and eventually advocating for himself. Marco understood very clearly that it was his job to explain his dip in grades and not his father's story to tell. He just needed time.

Consider your obstacles. Almost every teenager has something that feels like a barrier to success. Sometimes it is a known barrier, like with Marco, and others suffer from low self-confidence, a tough home life, depression, or a learning difference.

Colleges want fighters, students who have the wherewithal to keep moving forward, and those who are willing to advocate for themselves. Whatever barriers are in your way, I encourage you to prune them, and shape who you are. And when you do, you will shine!

Final Note:

You are only at the beginning of a full life's journey. Consider high school one huge tight rope with the biggest safety net underneath. That net is just waiting for you to fall and bounce right back up. You are resilient. You are amazing beyond your imagination. You are in control of you.

Just like Monday Morning Quarterback is meant to criticize actions and decisions of the past, I claim Self-Improvement Sunday. Get your team of supporters, village of cheerleaders, and community of believers and revise and adjust your plan to win!

You are now in the home stretch and ready to take control of senior year. You got this!

CHAPTER 6

YOUR SENIOR YEAR PLAN

TIP #23: Your list of colleges is key. The goal is to have choices in April.

TALE:

Listen To Your Counselor, Then Choose What's Right For You

Once the school day was done, I pulled Saige's file to review the compilation of notes. In short, Saige was a solid B student, with a couple of advanced placement courses, average test scores, and a good list of activities. A kid like Saige would have access to nearly every four-year college in the country, just not the highly selective ones. Her parents lauded her writing, while her teachers were kind but not overly enthusiastic.

With that said, I liked Saige. I liked the swagger in which she had walked in to my office early this morning and in all seriousness said, "Ms. Colón, I decided I want Dartmouth." Now it was my job to prepare a list of colleges, and she would only need to choose no more than ten. Easy.

"Congratulations on 'Student of the Week' for English," I smile. "Thanks, Ms. Colón."

"I know you want to discuss your early application to

Dartmouth, so we can do that first. Then I want to discuss your list of colleges. Sound good?"

"Sure. I have a list that I brought," Saige pulled out a sheet of notebook paper with a list of colleges. I acknowledged the list and left it on the desk.

We spent thirty minutes talking about her writing, fencing, and her work with School on Wheels and then narrowed a list of possible topics for her college essay. A smirk was about as big of a smile as I'll got from Saige , but I took this as a sign of trust.

"Let's take a look at your list."

- Duke
- Brown
- Stanford
- Northwestern
- Amherst
- Columbia
- UC Berkeley
- Vassar

"Saige, this is a very strong list of schools with excellent writing programs. What I want to do is come up with a few lists. Let's find a range of schools before we finalize. Sound good?"

For the first time, Saige shifted in her cushioned chair. The remainder of our time was spent in negotiations like two 4th graders exchanging lunch items from their lunch pail, "I'll give you my fudge stripes cookies for your bag of gummie bears."

Saige's second list consisted of schools like, UVA, New York University, and USC. I moved on to set up a new list trying to add Oberlin, University of Iowa, Hamilton, Colby, and Emory. Saige stared at my list, "Can we move Hamilton, Colby, and Iowa, to another list?"

"Saige," I looked directly at her, "My job is to make sure you have plenty of options this April. By moving these schools, there are no sure bets in the first three lists."

Just before winter break, Saige appeared in the doorframe of my office. Leaned against her left side, her golden ringlets hung in the gap between the frame and her shoulder. Her face–plain. Her emotion–sad.

"I was denied," she remained motionless.

I tilted my head to mirror her lean and said, "Oh, Saige, I'm so sorry." She stared through me and slowly pulled herself away from the door and into my office.

"I want to re-apply in regular decision," the moment of comfort was immediately stolen by her matter-of-fact tone.

"Saige, a deny means that they have eliminated you from their applicant pool," as loving as it sounded in my head, there was no way to kindly say those words to a teenager whose dream has just been punched in the face. I sat quietly and let her grieve her loss. It occurred to me for the first time that she *never* saw this coming.

A few weeks later, we picked the conversation back up. "How was your break, Saige?"

"Good. I worked to raise $500 for School on Wheels,"

Audra offered.

My nervous anticipation got the best of me, and I could not wait to ask, "How did it go with the applications? I only received your paperwork for your first choice schools."

"Oh. I didn't apply to the others. I don't really want to go to any of them." I was ill equipped to respond.

Saige set her sights high as so many do. Her broken heart from December did not allow her to see herself at any other place than that with which remotely resembled the Ivy League beauty and/or reputation.

"Saige, I don't know that you will get in to any of those schools. And now the January 15 deadline is in a week."

Saige shrugged her shoulders as if to say, "It's fine. No need to freak out."

Within five minutes of leaving my office, I printed a Common Application and personally delivered it to Saige in class and insisted she complete the application by Friday. The same day, I called her mother and spoke candidly about the real possibility that Saige would not be admitted to a single institution on her current list. Thursday morning, before the first bell, I had the complete application in hand. Saige had chosen ten schools that I was pleased with, and on her own had discovered Colorado, Manhattanville, and Whitman Colleges. Saige was sure to have choices in April.

TRUTH:

There are over 3000 four-year colleges and universities to

choose from in the United States alone. Do not, I repeat, do NOT set your heart only on the top 100. Do yourself a favor and

"Do not, I repeat, do NOT set your heart only on the top 100."

go back to chapter two of this book, and do your homework. Be open to new places, and find institutions that have the major you are looking for. To use a dating cliché, there are plenty of fish in the sea. If you are only fishing in one particular pond, you may come up short. Yes, captain, you are in control of your process, but do listen to your counselor. Counselors often have a suggestion or two that you have never heard of and could be a good match. All I am suggesting is that you give 1000 percent to the task of coming up with your list of colleges. If you can give it your all, you are sure to have multiple choices in April.

"Counselors often have a suggestion or two that you have never heard of and could be a good match."

TIP #24: Your authentic "why" brings authenticity to your college essay.

TALE:
Find Your Why And Thrive

What do you value? What is important to you? How do you begin to decide what to write about in the most important essay of your life? As your college counselor, I can help with this.

Among the first essay writing exercises is my favorite 15-minute "Values" exercise. Without much thinking, write down on a piece of paper the top three to six things that are most important in your life right now—today. Most students write down something that falls into the following categories: People, Athletics, Leadership, Service, Hobbies, Experiences, and sometimes, Objects. Examples include Grandma, basketball, cooking or film club, comic books, divorced parents, or a button collection. Even at the young age of 15 or 17 years old, you have likely experienced triumph, failure, hardship, heartbreak, rejection, and/or grief. There is plenty to write about that will give any reader a real peek into your life. But this takes time and thoughtful reflection.

It is easy to spot an essay from a writer who took the time to find their WHY. These three excerpts below come after several, and I mean more than three, drafts. Once you have decided on your top values (your "whats"), in the next column, write down WHY it is important to you. For students for whom a sports team is a value, it may be because it is a team sport where you have found your best friends. For others, it may be because of your growth as an athlete and dream of playing in college. These are two completely different essays. In the final column, write a brief sentence about a story that describes your "why."

Here are three examples of how the writer thrived once they found their WHY.

JAMES: Freedom to be Me (summer experience)

Armed with green hair dye and orange tempera paint, we set a date. We met on the grassy quad and 25 kids proceeded to paint my body, head to foot. There I stood, with brown shorts, turquoise curly hair, and orange paint cracking everywhere. Our activity coincided with Water Bottle Bongos and the Meditation Circle. Soon, the three groups merged and formed a chaotic clot of drumming, incense waving, and Jamba Juice sipping kids performing tribal dances and giggling with delight. And in the middle was one Oompah Loompah having the time of his life.

I remember James so well because he was uber smart. He came across as super serious and uncompromising. These qualities made him unapproachable to most of his peers. I was determined to crack him and figure out what makes him tick. His values included, academic decathlon, robotics team, and Center for Talented Youth. My immediate thought was this, "For where he is applying, everyone is smart and has these listed on their resumes. How do we make him come to life on paper?" He began drafting on Monday. After Tuesday's draft, I was still not overly enthused, proving that even the smartest kid in the room can write a dry essay. I took him outside and made him tell me story after story, until he finally cracked a smile. We found it. "Draft that story," I said and he looked puzzled. "Trust me, that is your 'why,'" and he followed my directions. This essay embodies the real James, and at the same time it shows the reader the kind of place James will fit in: where he will discover his people.

RICHARD: Ice Hockey in LA (athletics)

When my friends and I approached our athletic director, he immediately turned us down. Refused to be defeated, we began looking for a league to join. During this process, we discovered that the local professional team was looking to sponsor a high school hockey league. All we needed was $200 per player, and we would become a member of the league. There were two problems: first, we only had three players, but needed six, and second, we had no money to join.

. . .

We held tryouts, three players showed up, doubled our team, and a starting line up was born.

This would be a good example of how sometimes the sport

essay is not about playing the sport at all. It was clear when I met Richard that he loved ice hockey but hated that it was not a popular sport in Los Angeles. Richard knew everything, and I mean EVERYTHING, about hockey, and that summer I learned too. But what it boiled down to was how proud he was that he founded the ice hockey team at his school. In other words, his Value/WHAT was clear: Ice Hockey. His WHY was not about playing the sport but leaving a legacy of the sport he loved at the school he loved. The reader comes away from this essay understanding Richard's passion for the sport, his resilience to keep pushing forward, and his leadership qualities among his peers. Brilliant.

AUTUMN's Essay: Okefenokee Swamp (Travel with family)

The bow of our boat cut slowly through the murky, tea-colored water. The wet bark and lazy branches, bending down as if attempting to drink from the liquid, added to the ancient, mysterious aurora that permeated the swamp. As I looked around the boat, I suddenly remembered I was not living in the middle of a suspenseful and intriguing adventure story, but in the middle of my family's annual road trip.

...

Tony, the tour guide, went on to explain that Okefenokee came from the Native American for "land of the trembling earth." Looking around the boat at the faces of my family, the world felt surprising stable to me.

This is one of my all time favorite essays. When Autumn and I first began to work together, she had written in her first column, "Traveling to 47 states." When pushed on her "why," she said things like, "seeing the country," "exploring national parks," and "driving in the car for hours with her family." Boom, I thought, there it is. Her eyes lit up when she shared countless tales of her family's summer excursions across the US map from Grand Tetons to Acadia National Parks. Her WHY was not in fact about the thousands of miles she has traveled, but rather, the quality time she spends with her immediate family. This essay is one brief window of time in Autumn's life with her mom, dad, and sister. Autumn paints a clear picture of the kind of adventures she has experienced, but more than that, we understand that she values her incredibly close family.

TRUTH:

The truth is, at 17 years old, you have everything it takes to write a tremendous essay. The key is honing in on why you've chosen the topic. This essay is only one window for the reader

"You cannot fit everything into one essay, so remember to take my advice, "It's not what you value, it's about why you value it."

of your application to get a glimpse into your life. You cannot fit everything into one essay, so remember to take my advice, "It's not what you value, it's about why you value it."

If I'm being honest about the college essay, I must admit there are many that are written about sports. And they typically fell into three categories: failure, success, or from failure to success. It is not impossible to stand out with an essay about sports, but it is difficult. The biggest pitfall is making the essay too much about the entire team and not specifically about you. I cannot emphasize enough the importance to drill down your "why." If you read your essay and think, "This might be too generic," it probably is. The essays that stand out are the ones that give the reader a clear, concise, and correct picture of who YOU are, and nobody else. There is only one you. Find your authentic WHY and thrive!

TIP #25: The best essay topics are in you but not always obvious.

TALE:
Dig Deeper And Discover A Gem

School was never a top priority for Oliver. Without digging to hard, Oliver achieved decent grades and seemed satisfied with the results. Instead, he poured his energy into theatre and his love of books. Oliver was well read but savvy enough to know that while he was a straight B+ student, he needed an essay to help him stand out, which is what led him to my office.

I began with one of my prompts, "Describe for me what I would find on the walls and in the corners of your bedroom." Confused by what his counselor was asking but willing to indulge me, Oliver began. One wall was adorned with Notre Dame paraphernalia and complimented with an old map of the city of South Bend, prominently featuring the southernmost bend of the St. Joseph River, from which the city derived its name. Embarrassed a bit, Oliver admitted he owned Cubs bed sheets–his mother's and his favorite baseball team. His grandmother taught in the Chicago schools and hosted an annual family gathering at Wrigley Field, hoping against all odds that this was finally the year for the pennant. The long wooden dresser was an exhibit of small and large trophies Oliver had won while playing flag football, soccer, and later for acting competitions. After graduating from Notre Dame and St. Mary's College, Oliver's parents chased their dreams in Hollywood, CA. His mom had some success landing a few cameo roles as friend to Tracy Gold's character on the hit show, Growing Pains. "The top right hand drawer is reserved for all the programs of the plays I've acted in," Oliver smiled, and I thought we might be on to something, but without a beat he continued on with the final wall.

"In the corner, is my father's rocking chair next to the reading wall," his expression told me Oliver had saved the best for last. As a child, Oliver's father sat in the rocking chair before bed and Oliver selected a book. Even today it was Oliver's routine to sit and read each night. The bookshelf stood four feet tall, but the entirety of the exposed wall featured framed photos and postcards that Oliver and his father had collected. Curious, I dug deeper and prompted for more details. On a trip to Los Angeles, Mr. Sullivan took Oliver to his favorite bookstore, Book Soup, on Sunset Blvd. It was there that Oliver found a photograph of his favorite actor, Elijah Wood, reading a book. The photo was taken on the set of *Lord of the Rings*, with Elijah, dressed as Frodo, atop a tree reading the hard back book, *Game of Thrones*. Since that time, Oliver and his father made a habit of scouring bookstores, antique stores, and cathedral gift shops for similar photos. His favorite photo highlighted Walt Disney in a rocking chair with one daughter on each knee as he reads a book to them. I didn't have to prod, he continued describing other readers, Abraham Lincoln, Martin Luther King Jr., Marilyn Monroe, Albert Einstein, Hillary Clinton, Helen Keller, and Muhammad Ali. The collection was like his baseball trading cards. Oliver could name the city, state, date, and location of where he and his father had found each prized possession. It was pure joy to watch him recount each one.

There it was. Oliver had dug deeper than he ever had on any homework assignment. The category–people, the subject/topic– his father, the "why"–passing on the love of reading, the unique story–the photo of Frodo reading on set begins a tradition. Oliver left my office that day certain of one thing, not a single student in the applicant pool could replicate his essay. He dug deep and discovered his personal gem.

TRUTH:

Your college admission essay offers the admission officer a window into your life. Even a poorly written essay (and there are many) can stand out if the story is engaging. However, the most compelling essays are not only written well, but the story is unique, told in the student's authentic voice, and holds the reader's attention from start to finish. If you can carve out the

"The most compelling essays are not only written well, but the story is unique, told in the student's authentic voice, and holds the readers attention from start to finish."

time to take inventory of what stands out in your life as a high school student and what you value, then you are halfway there. Finding a topic is easy: People, Athletics, Leadership, Service, Hobbies, Experiences, and sometimes, Objects. The trick is to find the particular story that is unique only to you.

By in large, college essays are typically much too general and quite often are one-dimensional. What I mean by that is that just as movies are formulaic - boy meets girl, girl falls in love, something terrible happens, boy is reunited with his love in the end – college essays can feel the same way. For example, Oliver could have written his essay with this formula: dad reads to him as a child, Oliver falls in love with reading, a bookshelf of used books always reminds him of his father. A good essay, and yet you can see how by just digging a little deeper, there are layers and dimensions of Oliver we can gain by revisiting, revising, and revamping his essay for several drafts.

No pressure, but this is likely the most important essay you will write in your life thus far. Do not settle for one-dimensional. Do not settle for the first or second draft; push yourself to dig deeper.

TIP #26: Always ask for a positive letter of recommendation from your teacher.

TALE:

T-A-C: How to get the best out of your teacher!

The summer I spent teaching English to incoming freshmen, I taught them the formula to writing a body paragraph, including a topic sentence, analysis, and a conclusion sentence (T-A-C). I later stole that formula as a college counselor and showed students how they could consider T-A-C with regards to the letter of recommendations from their teachers, "Thinking about T for the thesis of the letter, A for their argument or supporting evidence, and C as the conclusion paragraph for the admission officer."

Consider for a moment the task of a teacher when s/he sits down to write a letter of recommendation. The teacher may have a great thesis statement but cannot recall the supporting evidence to support her claim. Or he might have one recollection of the fabulous paper you wrote about Madeline Albright as the first female Secretary of State but has no clue what you do outside of the classroom. We want to avoid this from happening by doing all the work on the front end. I have found the best letters of recommendation come when a student has taken the time to draft up his/her own T-A-C to give to each recommender.

Reflect on why you are asking this particular teacher to write your letter of recommendation. Most likely you have decided that s/he can highlight your skills in communication, writing, research, visual or performing arts, or math, science, or technology. This teacher might also be able to describe your qualities as a leader, athlete, or community builder. Being clear about what you believe your teacher can highlight is key in acquiring the courage to ask. Giving the teacher even one nugget in your initial request will almost always guarantee that the teacher will respond with an enthusiastic "Yes."

Matthew might say, "Mr. Baran, I was hoping you might agree to write my college letter of recommendation." Breathe. "I learned how to better communicate my arguments through the debates in your class. Do you think you could write a *positive* letter of recommendation about me?"

After a "yes" from one or two teachers, the hard work follows. Using an abridged version of the T-A-C formula, draft your own short essay about yourself for each teacher. Decide on two or three qualities you would like each teacher to highlight. Giving the teacher specific skills and qualities helps him/her contemplate additional positive examples of their own. The proof, however, is in the pudding. It is in the supportive evidence that you can offer a teacher that will ultimately infiltrate their minds as they write your letter. A stand-out letter is one that can convey strong anecdotal evidence to support a teacher's claim. The following are reduced examples:

For Matthew's Social Studies Teacher:

In your American history course, I became a better communicator by learning how to develop stronger arguments among my peers through the debate and discussions in your classroom. I was able to utilize those skills in my final paper, making a persuasive case of why Leroy Robert "Satchel" Paige is the best pitcher in baseball history.

For Matthew's Science Teacher:

Taking an introductory physics course with you as a freshman inspired me to join "Record Sea-ker," the school robotics team. As the moderator of that team, I learned from you how to build, program, and operate a real robot. I remember when "Seas the Day," malfunctioned last year at the FIRST competition. With your guidance, I was able to lead my team to collaboratively diagnose the problem and quickly repair the damage before the next elimination round.

You are now on your way to getting the best out of your teacher and submitting a quality application. Give yourself a round of applause!

TRUTH:

Not every college requires letters of recommendation. However, for those that do, they matter. Why? Each piece of the application–the transcript, test scores, personal essays, letters of recommendation, and possibly an interview–paints an additional piece of who you are as a student and as a human being. Consider each piece as quilting together the masterpiece of your life that authentically shares the story of you.

"If you can take the time to help your teachers, they will go out of their way to give you their best write-up!"

The craft of writing takes time and does not come easy for all teachers. If you can take the time to help your teachers, they will go out of their way to give you their best write-up! This exercise shows the teacher that you are professional and are taking the college admission process seriously. Exercise the control you have in all portions of your application, and you will be the better for it.

Extra TIP: What I like about this exercise is that it forces you to consider all of the portions of your life you want to reveal in the college application. By the time you are a senior in high school, there is little time to do much about your grades and test scores. What you have control over at this point are the two to five essays you will write and the counselor and teacher recommendations. Write down the five or six things you value most in your life–each on a separate sheet of paper. Marinate in those ideas for a day or two. Decide first what you will write about, and then allocate the remaining pieces to your recommenders. You will not only get the best out of your teachers, you will get the best application out of you!

TIP #27: Senior year is not for the faint of heart. Find a way to relieve stress and release fears.

TALE:
Lucky Ducks

The stress inflicted on you during the college admission process is real. Image playing in Game 7 of the World Series but having to wait several weeks to know the result of the game. Or consider going in to have a mole checked for cancer and having to wait months to receive an answer. At the age of 17, you hit the send button on an application that fades into thin air, to be read by someone you have likely never met, and you wait for a decision that comes months later. By the time the holidays arrive, as a senior, you finally realize that in less than 10 months, you will leave the comfort of your home and your friends, and be on your own. You might think that I am being overly dramatic, but do not underestimate your stress level. But do work to manage it.

At Marymount, it was Ms. Gergen who found a way for her seniors to relieve stress. It began with a story about a student who stumbled into Ms. Gergen's office the Friday before taking her SAT exam. The yellow rubber duck sat at the corner of Ms. Gergen's desk, and when she felt the stress Mary Jane was under, she took a chance and enthusiastically suggested that the senior rub the head of the duck. As the story goes, "MJ" rubbed and rubbed until she giggled about how silly she was about her nerves. She was completely prepared for the standardized test, and the little duck simply helped to channel the stress out of her and into the world. MJ did very well on her exam and had a variety of enviable college options in April.

That story took flight, and soon students took turns coming in to rub the head of Lucky Duck before a chapter test, a mid-term paper, or a final exam. Each year as students visited their first choice colleges, they brought home a Lucky Duck from their dream school. Ms. Gergen eventually put in several shelves and created big white collegiate columns wrapped in recycled Common Applications. As girls awaited their acceptance letters, they would pop into the office to visit their Lucky Duck in hopes of an extra special April.

Ms. Gergen had unconsciously created a space for students to release their stress and discuss real fears in an informal, yet healthy way. Around the shoebox shrine, the girls were free. What Lucky Ducks they were to have Ms. Gergen.

TRUTH:

I apologize in advance. I am guilty of being that admission officer that tried to tell students "Not to worry," "Don't stress," or "It will all work out." When I left college admissions for a job as

Director of College Counseling, my colleague said, "You are moving to the shipping side of the desk instead of the receiving end." I shudder at the thought of it now, but the truth is, when you

"To help you out I will offer a huge reminder to all Admission Officers: "Handle with care. Fragile package inside."

work on the receiving side of the desk, it is difficult to understand all that goes into a package before it is shipped. To help you out, I will offer a huge reminder to all Admission Officers: "Handle with care. Fragile package inside."

While I understand that there are no words that can calm your nerves while you await your fate, I do know that my stale words are as true now as they were then. Surprisingly, this crazy process does all work out in the end. Find your favorite, "Let it go," song and play it loud and proud. Take comfort in knowing that you have done everything within your power and control, the rest will take care of itself. When in doubt, rub the duck!

Extra TIP: As a family, find your own "Lucky Duck" activity. What can you do to help channel the stress, anxiety, and real emotions onto something else, while at the same time, having healthy and supportive

"Take comfort in knowing that you have done everything within your power and control, the rest will take care of itself."

conversations? If you can find a quality activity, it will save a lot of tantrums, crying fits, and nasty fights along the way. A very tall order, I recognize. You can do it!

Final Note:

If you have read this book, made your plan, followed your plan, and adjusted your plan, then your plan is already working. You have given 1000 percent to what you control

"Your new plan is around the corner, be sure to celebrate each and every victory along the way."

and now all that is left to do is wait patiently. Go out and enjoy the rest of senior year, you've earned it, and I could not be more proud!

Your new plan is around the corner, be sure to celebrate each and every victory along the way.

CHAPTER 7

YOUR NEW PLAN AWAITS ...

TIP #28: Treat every big envelope as if it were the only one coming.

TALE:
Big Plans, Big City

Emily was unconventional in her choice of Ivy-type schools. Instead of applying to "H, Y, P" (Harvard, Yale, Princeton), she choose to submit applications to "P, C, C" (University of Pennsylvania, Columbia, Cornell). These three schools were no less powerful, but had the one thing Emily dreamed of since middle school: excellent film programs. The illustrious list of alumni in top entertainment roles made U Penn Emily's top choice, but an acceptance to any one of the triumvirate would surely suffice. Some of her classmates tried talking her into applying to UCLA and USC, but Emily feared the fact that she did not come from entertainment royalty would keep her out of the two best film programs in Los Angeles. From the time she and her parents walked in to my office at the young age of 14, Emily was transfixed on the colorful college pennants that decorated the walls. Marymount High School was the perfect place for Emily's big plans and even bigger dreams.

As a freshman, she wasted no time and joined the Spanish club, became a retreat leader, and found a teacher with an interest in film and founded the film club. Her grandparents surprised her with a gift of two back-to-back spring break trips with Señora Valenzuela. As a sophomore, the group traveled to Costa Rica, where they visited Iguazu Falls. Emily took short video clips at every stop and later edited a short 5-minute film for everyone on the trip. And as a junior, the group visited five cities in Spain, where Emily insisted on only speaking Spanish for the entire trip and fell head over heels in love with the country. By the time she was a senior, she had perfected her accent and, as the student body president and lead ambassador of VSG, she was often asked to speak to groups of 7th and 8th grade girls and/or parents. She always began by saying, "Welcome to Marymount," followed quickly by, "Bienviniedos a todos." Emily's story of her academic growth in the classroom, as a leader on campus, and the opportunities she'd been afforded in the short time at Marymount resonated with so many young girls. Her joyful and genuine disposition won the hearts of everyone she encountered.

As part of the Film Club's spring annual "Shorts on the Lawn," Emily's short 3-minute video featuring her peers dancing in various locations on campus to the tune, "Happy," had become a hit. The admission office used it at events, and it was one of two videos she submitted with her film school applications. The second one told the tale of the ghost of Cantwell Hall, Malory Marone. Emily carefully crafted a tale that spanned generations of women, the story of a young girl's desire to fit in and the risks she took to stand out. The 12-minute short was a delicate balance of the bliss of being a teenager combined with the sting of cruelty among peers. It was perfection—raw, real, and in some ways, rebellious. She had won third place at the Los Angeles International Student Film Festival.

Just as we were settling into March, admission decisions began to arrive in the mailboxes and via email. The final week of March, Emily would walk in and hold up her big envelopes and celebrate each and every one. It was no secret that Monday, April 1, was an important day. I arrived early Tuesday morning and waited for Emily in my office. Her big blue eyes and brown bouncy locks entered with a smile, we celebrated the one big envelope and the three small envelopes went unspoken. While P, C, C had decided to pass on Emily, this final big envelope marked her seventh acceptance letter. If Emily was disappointed, sad, or even angry, I wouldn't know it. In my office, she maintained her joyful disposition and we debated among the choices in front of her.

Over spring break, Emily and her parents traveled east to the three schools she had narrowed it down to. The Monday following her trip, Emily showed up with two gifts for me, a soy chai latte, and in the opposite, hand she help up an NYU college pennant for my office. "I noticed this one was missing, Ms. Colón," and with that I knew Emily had found her home.

TRUTH:

Every year, hundreds—no scratch that—thousands of students are disappointed, parents are mystified, and even counselors are sometimes at a loss for words over denied decisions that come from above.

"Receiving a big envelope from any college is truly an honor. Celebrate each one as it is the greatest achievement to date. The truth is: it is!"

Yes, we could easily attribute the deny letters to the two Bs Emily earned in her high school career, or the slightly (and I mean slightly) lower test scores, or maybe her glowing "it" factor didn't come across on paper. It is natural to want to boil it down to just one thing that prevented the pearly gates from opening, but we will never know. The truth is there is no good answer but to say this, understand that at the very selective colleges there are more qualified students than there are spaces. As hard as rejection is to swallow, remember to celebrate each "big" envelope as though it is the only one coming. If you can do that, then you will see how easy it is to fall in love with any school where you chose to apply and who choses YOU back. Emily wisely chose to fall in love with the college that loved her back.

The college admission process is not always fair. There are several milestones in this process, cherish each and every one of them. Receiving a big envelope from any college is truly an honor. Celebrate each one as it is the greatest achievement to date. The truth is: it is! Congratulations! Now go eat ice cream!

TIP #29: Caution: even Small Mistakes can be Impactful in the Admission Process.

TALE:
A Bulb in Bloom

Sitting at the window, I got cozy with my warm soy chai latte ready to face the stack of red admission folders. Admission folders were ready for review once complete with the necessary components: transcripts, test scores, personal essay, and at least two recommendations including one from the counselor.

Next to the tall red stack was the multi-colored pencil bag I bought in Guatemala. Today I would use the pink and purple pens to take notes on each file: purple to highlight the academic qualities, "AQs," and pink to highlight the personal qualities, "PQs." Reading season is like braving the cold winters; one must hunker down, endure the short daylight, and await the bulbs to bloom. Today I was determined to find a few blooming bulbs worthy of sending home a "big" envelope before Christmas.

Paulina from a school in San Diego was the next file and within minutes, I knew she was the one. A competitive gymnast, she trained six days per week at the San Diego United Training Center (SDUTC). Though her father played Big 10 basketball, Paulina had inherited her small frame from her mother and so by the age of 6, a gymnast was born. Invited by the SDUTC to join their competitive team, Paulina had done well at local and regional competitions but was not nearly as successful on the national stage. The writing was on the wall last spring that she would not likely be recruited to a top Division I gymnastics program. As part of the spring break college tour with her school, Paulina landed at the front steps of Main Hall on a gorgeous spring day when the tulips were in full bloom. She fell in love with our campus almost immediately. The Rose Parlor windows looked out onto the front of the school where she could see the colorful tulips while sipping tea with cookies at 3 o'clock on any given day of the week.

I read her application with a grin on my face while the pink and purple pens went to work. With great AQs and interesting PQs, Paulina was surely headed for an early Christmas gift. As I turned the page, I gasped. There it was staring me in the face–a yellow post-it. The hand written note attached to the counselor recommendation simply said, "Call me." The counselor's recommendation lauded Paulina's academic accomplishments amidst her demanding gymnastics schedule. Mrs. Garwood praised her as one of the top students in the last five years and was clearly supportive of Paulina's application in our Early Decision (ED) process. Removing my glasses, I rested my head atop the cushion and stared at the ceiling. It was only 8am in California.

"Hello, Cynthia, thank you for calling," she paused. "I know that Paulina applied ED from our school and I wondered if, well, I wanted to ask if she had disclosed her recent indiscretion?" Mrs. Garwood shared that Paulina had recently allowed a physics classmate to copy her lab work. Her tone was sympathetic, "It was so unlike her, and I strongly encouraged her to disclose this information on her own, I'm sorry to hear that she did not take my advice." We agreed Paulina was a very strong candidate and was likely to be admitted, but the fact that she had not been upfront about her transgression would raise questions during the admission committee.

My enthusiasm faded. My blooming tulip suddenly had a hovering grey cloud. Ugh. One week later I found myself describing all of Paulina's AQs and PQs. "There's one more thing. The counselor left a post-it to call her." The silence was palpable. A hand-written note to call a counselor was so rare; each story behind a yellow post-it quickly became an urban legend. With six faces starring at me, I recounted the tale of Paulina's eagerness to help a classmate. While nearly everyone at the table agreed that this was not the worst-case scenario, the discussion quickly turned to the integrity of our office. Where do we stand on an issue of cheating? How do we feel about the fact that she did not disclose this information? What message would we be sending if we admitted her now?

What should have been an easy Early Admit, turned into a hold. Paulina would now have to wait until April 1 to receive a definitive decision from her first choice college.

Sure enough, Paulina was the first student I heard from in January. She spent winter break writing a one-page letter to our office. Paulina was contrite and clearly learned an even bigger lesson by delaying her apology. The once looming grey cloud turned to bright sunshine, and when Paulina opened her large envelope the maroon and silver confetti flew out onto her bedroom floor! She would soon have tea and cookies at 3 o'clock and overlook the tulips from the Rose Parlor.

TRUTH:

There are many colleges that ask for discipline information, and depending on the infraction, schools will report offenses. Should you find yourself having broken a rule (and who doesn't), you will want to educate yourself on what your school deems reportable. This does not typically include being tardy to class or detentions. When I was the Dean, we only reported suspensions.

"There are many colleges that ask for discipline information, and depending on the infraction, schools will report offenses. Should you find yourself having broken a rule (and who doesn't), you will want to educate yourself on what your school deems reportable."

The truth is, this was not a life-changing mistake. It did not keep me from advocating for an otherwise perfectly qualified student, but at the end of the day, cheating is cheating. Mrs. Garwood encouraged Paulina to do the right thing by taking ownership for her small, though impactful, mistake. Though I cannot know for sure, my gut tells me if Paulina had sent a separate note admitting her fault, this tale would not have made this book. Paulina would have received the large envelope before Christmas and that would be that.

If you learn nothing else from this tale, know this, if your counselor tells you to report it, write that letter immediately.

TIP #30: A wait-list letter is neither a yes nor a no.

TALE:
April Showers Sometimes bring May Flowers

Though rare, I thought I should shed light on the admission letter known as the "in limbo" letter. You are neither admitted or nor denied, you are simply in temporary limbo.

Candidate #1: Colette applied to only one Ivy League school for her love of their writing program. She had all the numbers, high grade point average, top ranked in her class, high SAT scores, and an 800 on the writing portion of the exam. Colette had given up competing as an Irish step dancer by the end of her sophomore year to dedicate her time to writing. Mrs. Miller had groomed her, and by senior year, Colette was editor in chief of the school newspaper and of the literary magazine. She had found her calling and won accolades for her opinion pieces and poetry. Colette had also recently taken a liking to being part of the tech crew for the performing arts productions. So when she was not working on her novel, you could find her behind the stage. Teachers raved about her and sent great letters of recommendation. Mrs. Miller lauded, "Colette is by far the best student I've had in my 25 year career as a teacher." There is no doubt the only thin envelope that read, "wait-list," was a shot to her ego. Though her desk was filled with acceptance letters from all over the country, this April shower rained hard on Colette's parade.

Collete's response:

As her college counselor, I called the admission office, "Diane, she is one of our finest, is there anything she can do?" Diane offered that her office had seen a huge increase in applicants, and she agreed that just one year before, Colette might not have been overlooked. She gave me hope, and I enthusiastically delivered my message to Colette, insisting she could write a letter reminding Diane (the Los Angeles representative) of why the college was her first choice, her most recent accolades, and how she would become a contributing member of the community. Colette wanted none of it. If they could not see how fabulous she was in the first round, she would not put up a fight. The shot to her ego was the bullet she accepted as her fate. Colette thanked me for my encouragement but went on to become a Wildcat at Northwestern in Chicago.

Candidate #2: William Friedman was from Scarsdale, New York, and attended a beautiful, sprawling campus. At first glance, William did not seem to fit the typical liberal arts applicant; he played football every fall and lacrosse in the spring. His most recent summers were spent in the city with coveted internships with Citicorp and CBS and wrote about his experiences in his essays. His desired major was listed as economics. William was definitely a student Vassar wanted, but compared to his private school counterparts, there were others who ranked higher and showed more compelling reasons why they were a fit for our college. To add complexity to our decision was the reality of where William's parents went to school. While there was no chance of William attending Wellesley College, where his mother attended, William's father attended Brown and worked as a senior partner at McKinsey & Company. Nearly every applicant in Vassar's pool also applied to Brown, and William was certainly no exception. At the end of the day, our office bet on the likeliness that his legacy status at Brown would win him an acceptance letter, and William would ultimately choose to follow in his father's footsteps. He received a wait-list letter from Vassar.

William's response:

What was not apparent was the fact that Vassar was indeed William's first choice. "Billy," as he preferred to be called, had followed his father's advice in academics and co-curricular choices. Instead of football, Billy longed to be on stage, had finally quit lacrosse and was currently in the spring musical. Billy planned to major in economics while also being part of the performing arts department. After receiving his thin envelope, Billy wrote the most incredible letter to our office with a new unfolding of who he was, who he aspired to become, and how he would learn from his peers at Vassar. Whatever held him back from sharing his true passions in his application was now set free. It was clear that Billy was not his father and now I had a reason to fight for him. Before the end of May, Billy was offered and accepted his spot at Vassar.

TRUTH:

Each year, the landscape of admissions for any given college is different and cannot be predicted. I remember one year we had room to admit nearly 20 students off the wait-list. On the other hand, one year we were over enrolled by early May and could not take a single candidate off the wait-list. With this in mind, understand that a wait-list is not a no, it is, however, a no until further notice.

YOU are your own presidential candidate. It is your job to give the voter, in this case, the admission officer, a compelling reason to say, "Yes! I'm voting on her/him."

"You cannot afford to be humble in this process; this is the one time you have permission to boast about yourself."

My emphasis here is on the word compelling. As the applicant, this is your chance to be authentically you and at the same time, persuasive.

If you can consider every application as though the institution had only one vote (no matter how selective the college), this should be motivation enough to create the most convincing application you can. It could mean the difference between getting admitted or wait-listed. In either case, you cannot afford to be humble in this process; this is the one time you have permission to boast about yourself. My hope for you is that you will not have to wait until May to bring your well deserved flowers. So make a strong case, and you will earn your big envelope in April.

TIP #30: Choosing a college is your decision. Just because your parents went there doesn't mean you have to.

TALE:
A Darker Shade Of Scarlet

"Shall we flip a coin?" I smugly suggested. Bobby dwelled upon his decision for over a week. "How about rock, paper, scissors," my jokes were no longer funny, and he simply wanted someone to put him out of his misery.

"Come on, Dr. Colón, I need your help." Bobby was desperate, and so I used an exercise I often used with the girls at Marymount. I drew three columns and made four rows. Across the top I listed the two Big 10 schools Bobby was deciding between, and asked, "Should we list one more for good measure? How about my favorite LA school?" Bobby agreed and for the first time in two weeks he cracked a joke, "Well at least I know I'll be wearing a shade of red one way or another."

I asked Bobby to list the things that were most important to his college experience. He quickly rattled off, "Business major, sports medicine for student interns, opportunity for study abroad, and school spirit." Each of these was transcribed into the rows on my left. Bobby's job was to rank each school by the criteria on the left.

"Now, of the four criteria you gave me, rank them in order of importance to you," I didn't really have to ask, at his core, Bobby could not wait to major in business. In addition, Bobby led St. Bernard's sports medicine program and "lived" on the field for every home and away game. He read books on the bus rides, completed homework in between games, and was up until one in the morning nearly every school night.

Bobby wanted nothing more than to continue his work on the sidelines, like his father, Michael Thompson, did in college. Bobby's big plan was to double major in business economics and exercise science as an undergraduate and later attend a top business school and become a sports cap analyst for one of his favorite NFL or MLB teams. Bobby's grandfather, known as "Papa Jack," spent his career as the medical doctor for the Cleveland Browns, while his grandmother, "Grandma (Mi) Chelle" worked in the ticket office for Cleveland Indians after she raised the twins, Michael and Mary. When Bobby's father told stories of his childhood, Bobby couldn't imagine a better life than "living" on a field.

Staring at the yellow pad of paper, Bobby knew in an instant the calculation I was about to make. Multiply the column ranking by each of the criteria ranking. For example, Bobby ranked business as his most important factor, earning the row labeled "Major" as No. 1. Across the row were columns A, B, C, which happen to be listed in order that Bloomberg Businessweek ranked the best undergraduate business schools; therefore, Kelley School of Business earned a 1, Max Fisher College of Business earned a 2, and Marshall School of Business earned a 3.

His heart raced, "Wait, the school with the lowest score is where I should go, not the highest, right?" Bobby's logical and analytical brain beat me to the punch. With a nod from me he stood and paced the floor, "But Papa Jack wants me to go to Columbus and continue the family legacy. I'll never make it on the field as a freshman. Football is too big there. I want hands on experience on the field." It was as close to him saying, "I don't want to go there," as I had heard from Bobby in nearly a full year. I knew what his top choice was and so did his gut; his logical brain was finally catching up.

"So what are you saying, Bobby?" I waited in silence for his decision.

"I'm going to be a Hoosier!" He smiled the biggest smile and gave me a high five!

Bobby went on to have a grand time at every season with football, basketball, and baseball. Papa Jack, Grandma Chelle, and his parents all traveled with Bobby whenever possible. They all proudly wore crimson and cream. Bobby discovered that his very own field of dreams was just a darker shade of scarlet.

TRUTH:

When I recruited for Vassar College, I presented to rooms

filled with students and parents. One of my favorite jokes to tell was that the list of colleges you are applying to often (if not always) contained the colleges where your parents attended at the top of the list. The nervous laughter in the room always told me that I was correct. I gently reminded parents that they had

"I know that telling your parents that their alma mater is not your first choice, or worse, that it is the last choice on your list, is not easy. Find a moment to be up front and honest about where your heart is and why."

their turn in college, and now this was their child's future at hand. And with that piece of advice, students, like you, exhaled. I am giving you permission to say, "I want to choose what is best for me."

I know that telling your parents that their alma mater is not your first choice, or worse, that it is the last choice on your list, is not easy. Find a moment to be up front and honest about where your heart is and why. Start with, "I don't want to hurt your feelings. I love your school. I am just not sure it is the right one for me." Or you can always say, "I want to make you proud. I found a school that I know I will love as much as you love your college."

TIP #32: Number two is sometimes number one.

TALE:
Big Jess, Big Love

I don't think there was a single A- on her transcript, just straight As across the board. The only reason she was salutatorian of our class was because Dan had taken just one extra honors class our freshman year. On the day it was announced, Jessica went right up to her four-year arch nemesis and put her hand out for a firm hand shake and said, "Congratulations, Dan, you deserve it!" The grade point average may have selected him as valedictorian, but to everyone else in the class, "Big Jess" was everyone's number one.

Involved in *everything* on campus, Jessica became known as "Big Jess" when she sang a solo at an assembly in the spring of freshman year, and brought the house down. "That gurl got some BIG lungs," Brenda said and Head Cheerleader, Keisha agreed! At practice the next morning, Keisha announced "Big Jess" as the cheerleader of the week, and so it stuck.

Jess knew everyone's name in a class of 300. Big "GOOOD

Mornings" and big hugs were given out everyday. Jess was a perfect cross between hometown beauty queen and high school nerd. She treated everyone equally, and that's what made her so special.

I don't know if Jess knew how every senior was rooting for her to be admitted to her first choice college, UCLA. She had been limited to applying to public schools in California, with the exception of a few private Christian colleges where she was eligible for large scholarships. UCLA had been her dream since sixth grade, and Bellflower High had not had an acceptance there for three years. When she was admitted, news spread throughout the campus, and students, teachers, administrators, and even the maintenance staff stopped to give a hearty, "Congratulations." Certainly her father had shared the story to anyone who would listen back at the school district's maintenance staff headquarters. Just before spring break, Jessica's mom, Mama Leslee, sent in the deposit to UCLA, and she was officially a Bruin! As best friends, we would become cross-town rivals.

The final weekend in April, Big Jess attended Azusa Pacific University's "Cougar Pride" event as a guest of former BHS choir singer, Yuriko. While APU had offered a full tuition scholarship, the room and board was still more costly than UCLA. More than that, Jessica believed UCLA was the best choice for her future. Friday night, they hung out in the dorms and all of Yuriko's friends remembered Big Jess from a fall visit. The next day, they went to the spring festival, met other newly admitted students, and Jess was invited to join in with the choir that evening. Yuriko and Denise took Jess to the local "Doughnut Man" shop where at 1a.m. the line was around the corner. The three sat in the common room of the residence hall eating their Tiger Tail doughnuts until four o'clock in the morning. Among other topics, the girlfriends shared candidly about family, faith, and their future. At Bellflower High, Big Jess had all the answers, but somehow here in the quiet city of Azusa, she had found more questions.

Sunday morning, APU's Dean led chapel and began by saying, "I woke up this morning and scrapped my talk, for God has a different message for one of you in this audience." Big Jess will never quite remember what the Dean spoke of, but she can still feel the warm tears drip down her cheeks. She went to bed just six hours earlier questioning her life, her decisions, her faith, and woke up to have all her answers revealed in his 15-minute talk.

At 2 p.m., Mama Leslee picked up her daughter and Big Jess waved good-bye to five of her new best friends. She hardly spoke a word on the fifty-minute drive home. What to do? What about the deposit? How will we be able to afford this? Can I do this? Leslee turned on the radio and let her daughter contemplate.

Just before her father and brother arrived home from volunteering at the church, Jessica came out of her room, stood in front of the television to meet her mother's eyes, and said, "I'm supposed to go to APU. That is where I'm supposed to be." Mama Leslee stood up to embrace her daughter and confidently replied, "Well, if that is what you want, we will find a way."

Big Jess had the strength of a goddess. She did not care

what anyone said or thought about her decision, and I knew not to try and convince her otherwise. Once she made a decision and her family supported it, it was a done deal. Nothing anyone could say would change her mind. There is much satisfaction in being able to say for the rest of her life that she was admitted to UCLA, but not nearly as much satisfaction as saying she is an alumna of Azusa Pacific University. APU will forever be the place where Big Jess felt Big Love.

TRUTH:

This process can play with your head. To the outside world, you may seem perfectly calm, cool, and collected, but I know this is cause for much

"The college admission process calls on you to make your first real adult decision."

anxiety and stress. The college admission process calls on you to make your first real adult decision. This is hard stuff for anyone, so do not beat yourself up if you are struggling to make a final choice. I encourage you to tune everything else out and listen to what is inside your heart and soul. Whether it is your gut, your intuition, your god, or your higher power. Somewhere inside you knows exactly what to do. Allow yourself enough time make a decision, even if you change your mind five times. Once you know (you'll know when you know), voice what that is and don't

"Whether it is your gut, your intuition, your god, or your higher power. Somewhere inside you knows exactly what to do."

look back. Soon you can get on to enjoying your final weeks with family and friends.

TIP #33: Follow your heart—only you know where you are headed.

TALE:
Red Wings

Top of the 5th, no outs, and the star pitcher just walked the third batter. Time. Coach, catcher, and infielders huddle up on the mound. Vesta watches her son shake his head from her usual spot on the bleachers. Only she knows her son's confidence level and watches Scott wave off the coach with a simple, "I got this." With a tug at his ball cap, coach returns to the dugout while the crowd holds their breath. Batter number four takes a few warm up swings as the young man in pinstripes brings his glove and ball close to his chest. In a blink, we hear what sounds like a loud hiccup or short dog bark, indicating "Strike 1." Two more strikes follow in an instant. One out. Breathe. Vesta looks around and recognizes some of the NCAA baseball scouts in the crowd. Her eyes move back on the mound to watch her son. Scott doesn't like the catcher's suggestion, "Try again," he motions, and then closes his glove around the ball and "boom," batter number five swings, his bat unscathed. Scott delivers two curve balls and just like that, two outs. Bases still loaded, one more out to go. Breathe. Vesta knows what's coming, the four-seam fastball is Scott's specialty, and he has been known to clock nearly100 miles per hour with his secret touch. She holds back her giggle as batter number six takes the plate. The umpire squats down, watching the strike zone, and "bang," strike one, followed by an immediate, "boom," strike two. The batter has not swung the bat yet and holds out his hand to take a pause to re-group. The crowd is unbelievably quiet: no movement, no chatter, all eyes on the pitcher. Scott closes his glove around the ball, brings it close to his chest, looks back, looks front, and in one sweeping motion, the nine-inch ball with red wings flies off his fingers and punches the back of the catchers glove. The backspin is too much for the batter. Three outs, no runs, bottom of the fifth, the game is scoreless.

Scott went on to pitch the remainder of the game and the Buccaneers won. It was still early in the season, and as a junior, this was his time to shine. Though Scott received most of the attention in the local papers, he was the kind of kid who always gave "props" to his teammates in nearly every interview. He noted a great throw made by the shortstop or a tough catch by the outfielder, and Scott always thanked the catcher and the head coach. Reporters loved him and followed his career even before his varsity year as a freshman.

As a sophomore, Scott was already being heavily recruited and winning high praise in the papers. That October, Scott watched in awe as the Minnesota Twins won their second World Series Championship. Two months later, Scott opened his mail on a balmy Christmas vacation day, and there it was—a cream colored card with only one recognizable image. The gold embossed trophy stared at Scott as his index and middle fingers traced over each of the individual pennants. The inside only read this, "Merry Christmas ... The Minnesota Twins."

Scott's mom beamed with pride at every game, but at home, she was clear about her expectations; school always came first. If her son could put that much effort into his pitching, surely he could do the same in his studies. Her parenting paid off, and Scott was in the top 15 among our class of 300. Vesta's son was not only being recruited by some of the top baseball programs, but some of the best colleges around the country came to watch his fastball. Scouts came from Texas, Rice, Notre Dame, USC, UCLA, and ASU. Scott was not a fan of Texas, nor did he think he would survive the cold of the Midwest. If he had to decide at the end of that perfect-pitched day, it was be a coin toss between UCLA and ASU. Two names: Jackie Robinson and Barry Bonds.

At the end of his junior year, the baseball season came to an end when the Bucs battled an old local rival in the championship game. Scott left the game after pitching five innings, giving up only two hits and one run. The Bucs were leading 3-1, and the relief pitcher just needed six outs. 3-2 at the bottom of the 7th inning, man on 1st and 3rd. With a hard swing, La Mirada's best player hit a double and the outfielder chased the ball. They easily tied game, but the second runner came flying past third base in an attempt to beat the ball at home plate. Just as the Buc fans yelled, "Out," the umpire called, "Safe." Game over. Bucs lost.

The loss did not slow down the press and the interest in Scott's career. He was now discussed as a potential draft pick. Scott was well aware of the competitive talent and knew he would not be drafted within the first 20 or 30 rounds; his eye was still on college.

As a senior, Scott committed to Arizona State University, to follow in the footsteps of Barry Bonds and other greats like Reggie Jackson. Scott had one motto, "Win as much as I can and play as long as I am able." In his final year, Scott and his teammates finally won the CIF Championship title. This time, the young man in the maroon pinstripes pitched all seven innings, giving up only three hits and one run.

In June, Scott faced a tough decision. Now drafted in the 41st round, he had a choice. To his friends, the choice was obvious; take the scholarship and play ball in four years. Scott was not so sure. At the age of eight, he had fallen in love with a nine-inch round ball with tiny red stitching. It is the raise of the 88 inches of waxed red thread that acts as wings each time it rolls from the fingers of a talented pitcher–flying over 90 miles per hour. The euphoric feeling Scott gained each time the ball left his fingertips kept him coming back for more. For Scott, the obvious choice had been clear for ten years.

The gold and maroon ASU college pennant that now hung in his bedroom would soon be replaced with a red and blue pennant that bore the recognizable logo, "Twins."

TRUTH:

If you shoot for the moon, you will land on your star. Your star is unique, and only you know when you have found your home. Choosing a path to explore professional baseball, culinary arts, a career in dance, or design school, is just as impactful to your life's journey as going to college.

"The moral of this story is simple: at the end of the day, you are in control of your destiny and because you have planned it that way, you will have choices."

Scott did everything right. He followed an academic plan, athletic plan, and leadership plan. The moral of this story is simple: at the end of the day, you are in control of your destiny and because you have planned it that way, you will have choices. If your heart ultimately leads you on a path other than college, then listen. Only YOU know where you are headed.

Final Note:

Congratulations! One thousand times, congratulations. You are headed exactly where you are meant to be. This is an exciting time in your life. Get your team of supporters, village of cheerleaders, and community of believers and go celebrate!

AFTERWORD

For any high school senior, April is filled with extreme highs and extreme lows. Looking back on my own life, April has also served as a point of complete elation and severe heartache.

April served as the month I received my first job offer with Vassar, and four years later, I accepted my position at Marymount High School. Both experiences elicited emotions of pure joy.

And in complete contrast, some of the people who have mattered the most to me have April birthdays, but for various reasons, they are no longer in my life. I regret this on a few fronts, but I also know that sometimes people come in or out of your life for a very specific reason.

On April 12, 2014 we laid my father, Benjamin G. Colón, to rest. He was sixty-two years old. One year later, I was in the final stages of signing paperwork to file for divorce. Death and divorce kicked me in the pants and brought me to my lowest point.

In April of 2016, I was on Easter break, and in the quiet space of my head and my home. I had no choice but to face what I had avoided for nearly one year: myself. That week, I woke up every morning to my new routine: rise out of bed, read daily prayers, and get outside. I ran the streets of West Hollywood and Beverly Hills and hiked the trails of Griffith Park, all while listening to my new "girl power" play list. I did anything to keep busy and to keep from crying, but, the harder I ran, the harder I cried. What was I to do? I would not allow the pain of the last 24 months to define me, but I was determined instead for that deep cut to inspire my best self.

I began to write. At first it was thirty minutes, but then I could write for hours. It was cathartic. I uncovered old journals, found what I called "Dean Diaries," and gawked when I discovered my weekly entries in my first year as principal. I even found old speeches I had delivered in high school. I used everything for inspiration and kept writing.

A running routine provided time to think and listen to my inner voice. Somewhere along the way came the title "Tips, Tales, and Truths." But what did that look like? At first, each was its own section. The idea continued to evolve, and I continued to write.

As my Saturday morning run merged from Santa Monica Blvd. onto Melrose Place, I couldn't wait to get home. I walked into my condo, my turquoise running tank damp with sweat, and my fluffy malti-poo, Elvis, jumped onto the couch to welcome me home. I grabbed a tall glass of water and sat in my inspiration chair on the balcony. The Picasso-esque chair is my favorite gift from my father, and on this day, I knew he was present. Resting my legs up on a chair in front of me, Elvis curled up between my feet. I wrote and wrote until *Tips, Tales & Truths for Teens* was born.

I am a first generation college graduate. My parents had no idea how to help me access a four-year institution, but they supported my dream. How I ended up working at some of the most elite institutions is kind of crazy. Working at Barnard,

Vassar, attending Columbia, and guiding the girls at the exclusive Marymount opened my eyes to a world I did not know existed. Through those experiences, I realized just how unprepared I was when I attended USC. Talk about level playing field – mine wasn't even close. Thank God I was oblivious to this fact at the time.

Tips, Tales & Truths for Teens emerged because of a simple goal: to bring the knowledge I have had the privilege of experiencing to the masses. Who would I be if I did not otherwise serve all of the communities from which I come from and those of which I have experienced? This is a calling, a duty, and an expectation for myself to inspire as many students as possible to discover just how big they can dream. While I acknowledge that college is not the path for everyone, I completely believe that it is my education that has opened so many doors.

Both my mother and father instilled in me tremendous self-confidence that I did not appreciate until now. In my darkest days, I had lost that strong sense of self, but it is through this project that I found my authentic self, my authentic voice, and my authentic why. My April 2017 ended with complete elation and joy, when this book was finally complete. Now I can eat ice cream.

I sincerely look forward to hearing about your April celebrations to come! Hugs, love, and sunshine to you always.

Sincerely,

Dr. Cynthia Colón
www.drcynthiacolon.com

FINAL WORDS

You might recall that the counselor character in chapter one is named Mr. Vargas. In actuality, the character is inspired by someone I fondly call a champion of students, Mr. Raul Vargas. My mother and I met the founding director of the Mexican American Alumni Association (now known as Latino Alumni Association) in the fall of 1989. His personal mission statement was that of the organization: help as many underrepresented, first generation, low-income Latino students access the University of Southern California. He believed with all his heart that this very act would serve to better oneself (the student) who would eventually go on to achieve great things to better others (his family, her community). I can only pray that nearly 28 years later, I am finally fulfilling my duty to pay it forward.

Using Mr. Vargas as inspiration, I came up with the motto—fueling confidence, building dreams. Following in his footsteps, I am committed to supporting student scholarships at five schools that have always believed in my dreams. To learn more about each of these institutions and/or about how you too can help in fueling confidence and building dreams, please go to www.drcynthiacolon.com and click on the tab labeled GIVE BACK. I thank you for your support.

Made in the USA
San Bernardino, CA
17 August 2017